from Chihuly's Collection

Chihuly's PENDLETONS

and their influence on his work

Portland Press

Library of Congress Cataloguing-in-Publication Data
Chihuly, Dale
Pendelton / with an introduction by Charles J. Lohrmann
p. cm.
Includes bibliographical references
ISBN 0-000-000-0
1   Chihuly, Dale, 1941-
2   Art Glass–United States–History–20th century
I   Title
DC000.000000 2000
000.00 - 00

Published in 2000 by Portland Press, Seattle
First Edition

Contents

Collecting Trade Blankets

I started collecting Pendleton blankets in the late 1960s. I tend to refer to all trade blankets as Pendletons, even though there were dozens of manufacturers of these beautiful blankets. Some companies were large and others very small—and some existed for only a few years and others for an extended period—but only Pendleton, the most prolific and successful of the trade blanket manufacturers, still exists. Of course, there are new makers that come and go. The blankets are called trade blankets because they were originally made especially for the Indian market. The Indians would go to trading posts near or on the reservations and trade their own woven blankets, baskets, furs, and other goods for the machine-made blankets provided by the non-Indian manufacturers. ■ The Indians were willing to trade their extraordinary handwoven blankets for the trade blankets because they found these commercially produced pieces to be more colorful and warmer than their own blankets. They also valued the beauty of the trade blankets. From an economic point of view, one of the Indian handwoven blankets was worth several machine-made Pendletons. ■ We know very little about the early designs of the trade blankets. My collection now contains seven hundred different designs, and there must be at least that many more that I don't yet have. Some designs may have been lost forever—probably hundreds. What's truly fascinating to me and other collectors is how incredibly beautiful, aesthetically successful, and varied the designs and colors of these blankets are. There's considerably more variety in the trade blankets than in the Indian-made blankets, and that's another reason Indians wanted to wear and collect them. To this day, more trade blankets are sold to Indians than to non-Indians, and the Pendleton Company seems to give priority to the Indian outlets. The real mystery for me concerns the designers of these blankets. I believe the most extraordinary designs were done in the early years, between 1875 and 1915, and most of the designs since that time are in large part derived from the early pieces. The early designers were so creative that they seemed to exhaust most of the motifs and possible color combinations. It became more and more difficult to come up with truly original designs that reflected Indian themes. The early trade blanket designers probably didn't truly understand what many Indian designs meant or symbolized, or how the blankets functioned. ■ The Indian blankets were made to be worn in a variety of ways. When the blankets were worn, how the designs and patterns met and overlapped, had great significance. Not under-standing all of this gave non-Indian designers much more opportunity for

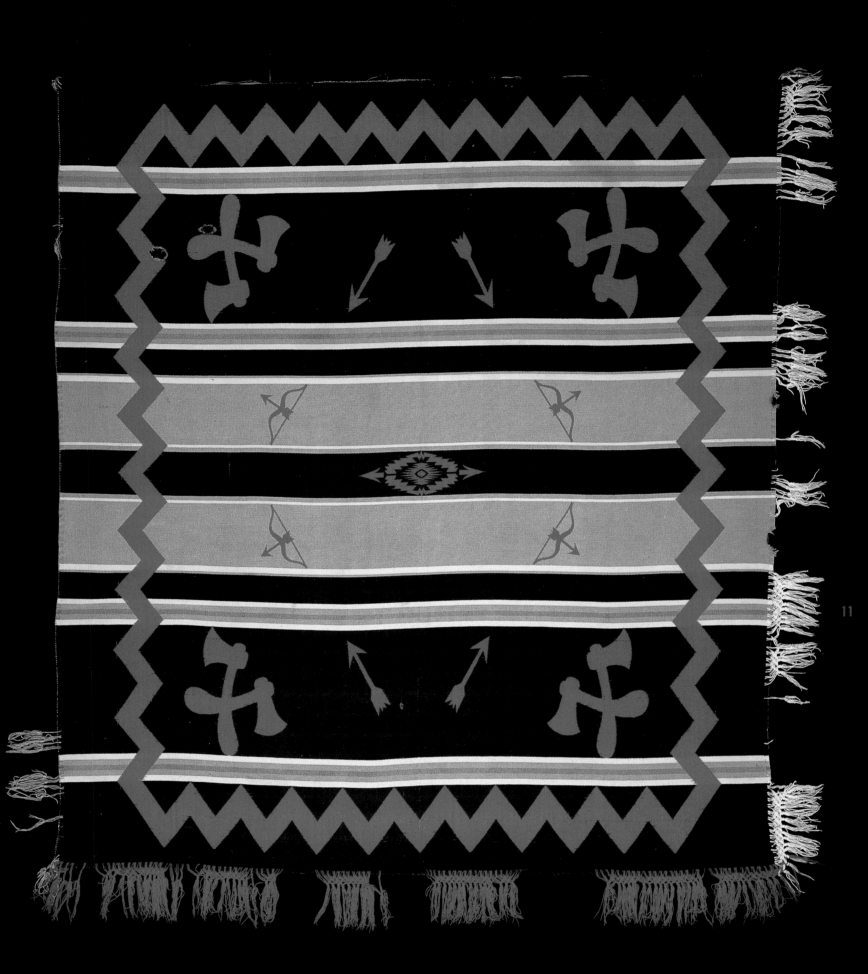

design variation and design freedom. For example, the amazing variety of yarn colors available to the factory designers (far more than the Indians used) was very important. It's wonderful to see turn-of-the-century designs using hot pink and chartreuse juxtaposed. The Indians would never have used this color combination, but they were very attracted to these bright and truly original color combinations that they had never seen before (and in some cases had never before been put together by any other culture). ■ A very important design feature that made the trade blanket totally different from the handwoven Indian blanket was the double weave that reversed the design of the blanket from one side to the other. If you had a blanket that had green crosses on a red field, when you turned it over it would have the opposite coloration—red crosses on a green field. There were actually two layers of design, and these two layers of yarn made the trade blankets extremely warm. This double weave was possible because of the sophisticated Jacquard looms that the manufacturers used. The loom had been invented by J. M. Jacquard in France around 1800. Without this invention and its introduction to America, the trade blankets would not exist. ■ The Jacquard loom was way ahead of its time. It operates somewhat like a player piano, another very advanced design for its time. The designer could create almost any design imaginable, and it would then be translated into a series of punch cards with holes in them, which the yarn would be threaded through. The designs could be (and at times were) extremely complicated, but once the cards were programmed and placed in the proper order of threading, the entire weaving of the blanket was totally automated with very little labor involved. Hundreds of blankets a day could be made on each Jacquard loom. All you needed was yarn and a Jacquard loom to open for business, and many did. ■ My main purpose in creating this book has been to illustrate the beauty and variety of the trade blankets. Most people interested in Native American art and/or textiles are familiar with the great Navajo Indian blankets, some of the most sought-after and beautiful weavings in the world. But far fewer people are aware of the trade blankets—textiles directly influenced by the Navajo blankets but not direct copies of them. Those of us who know and collect trade blankets feel that many of them are as beautiful as some of the great Navajo pieces. I hope the quality and attention paid to detail in this book will help to increase awareness of the splendid variety of the trade blankets. I hope you enjoy going through the book as much as we've enjoyed producing it.

■ Sincerely, Chihuly

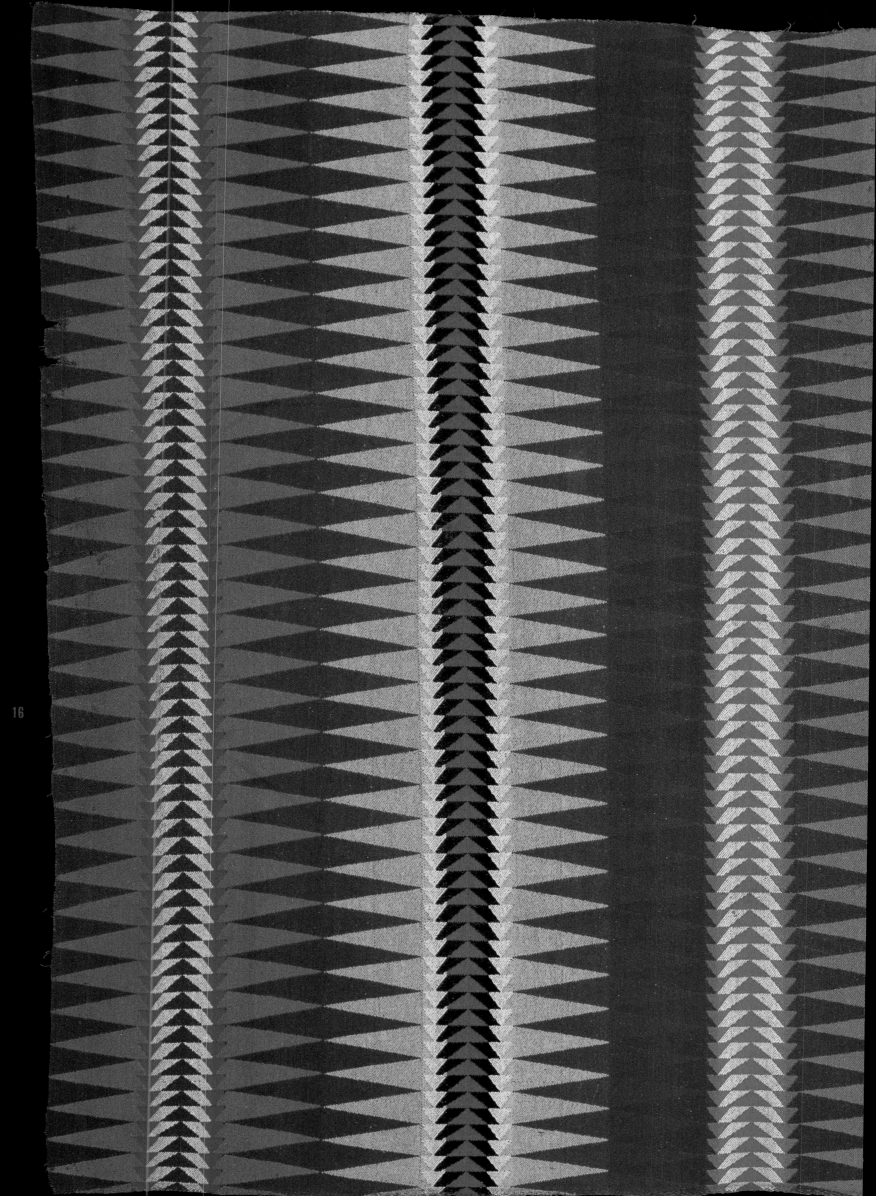

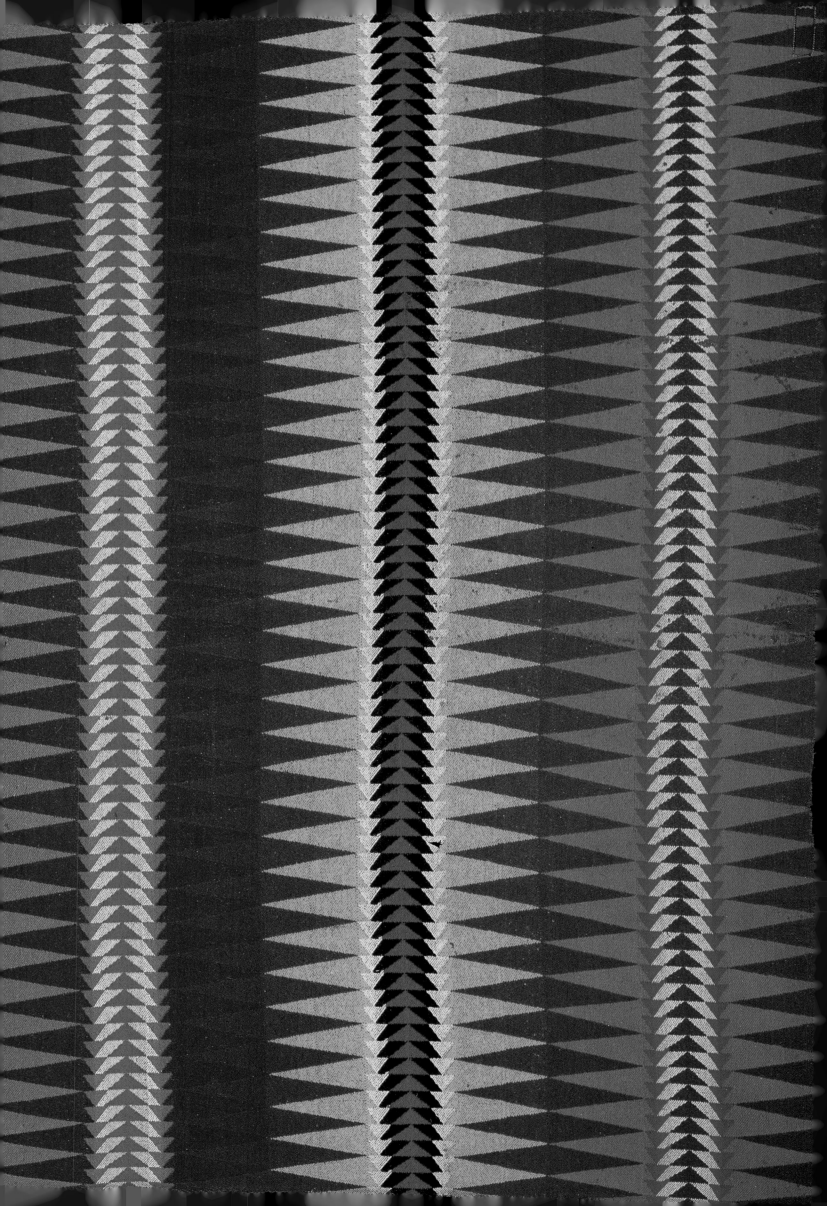

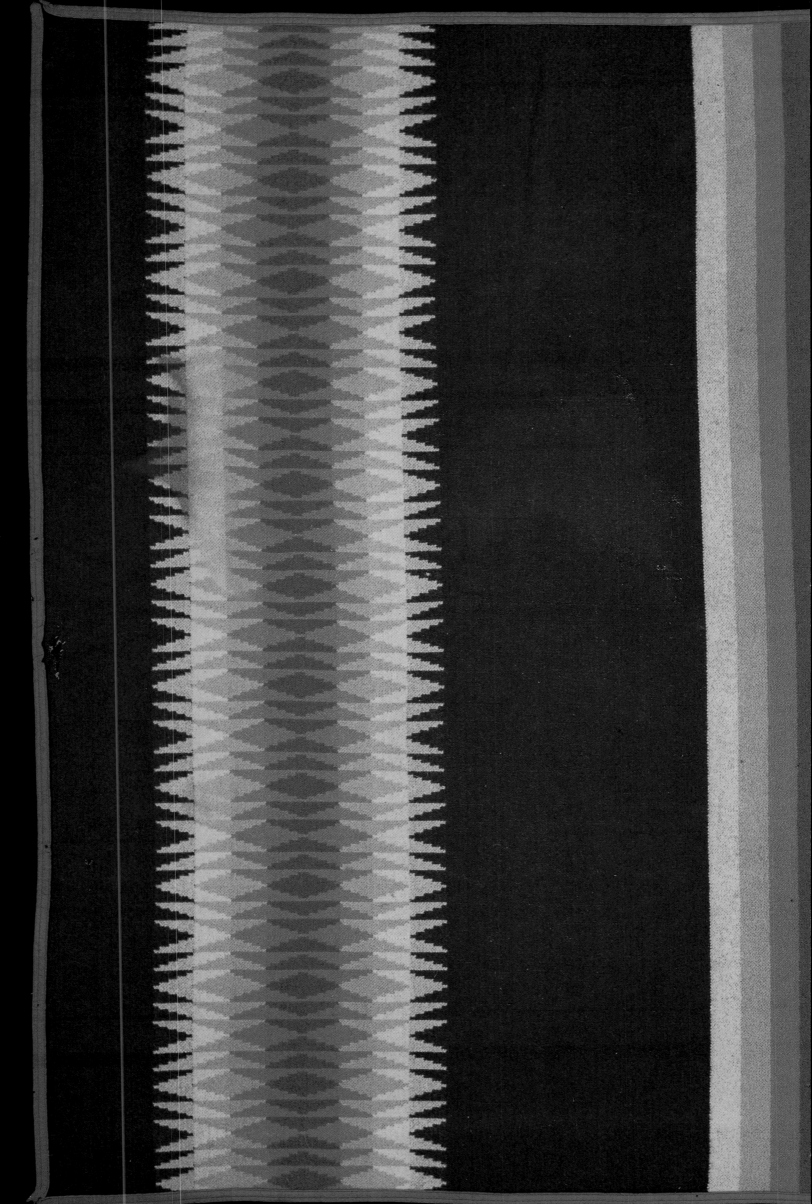

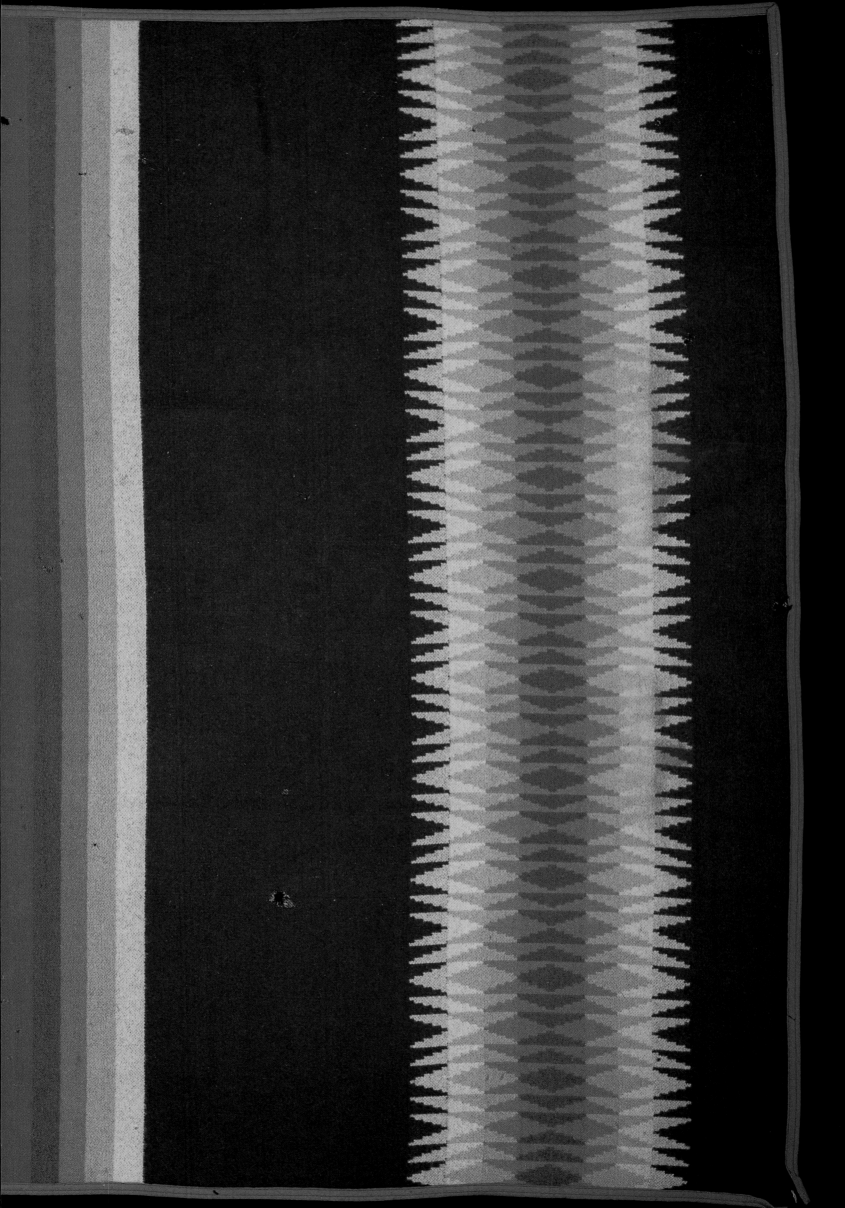

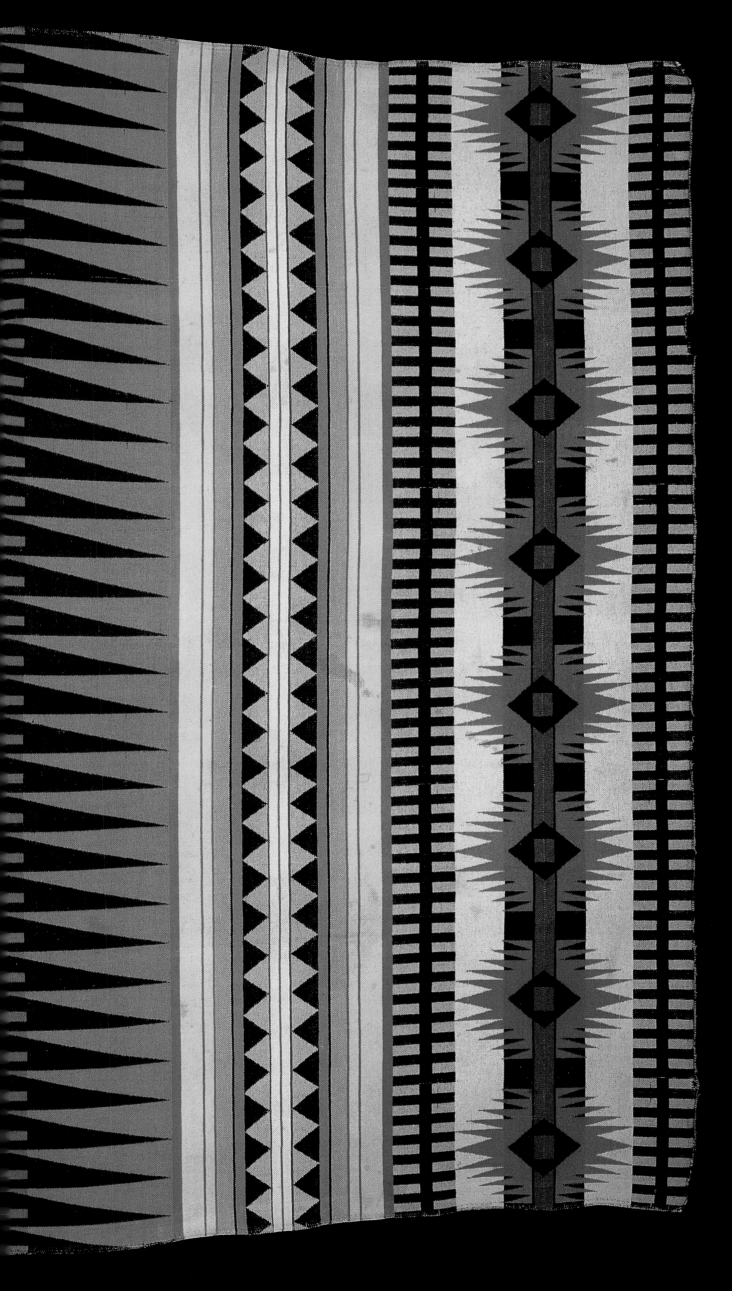

27

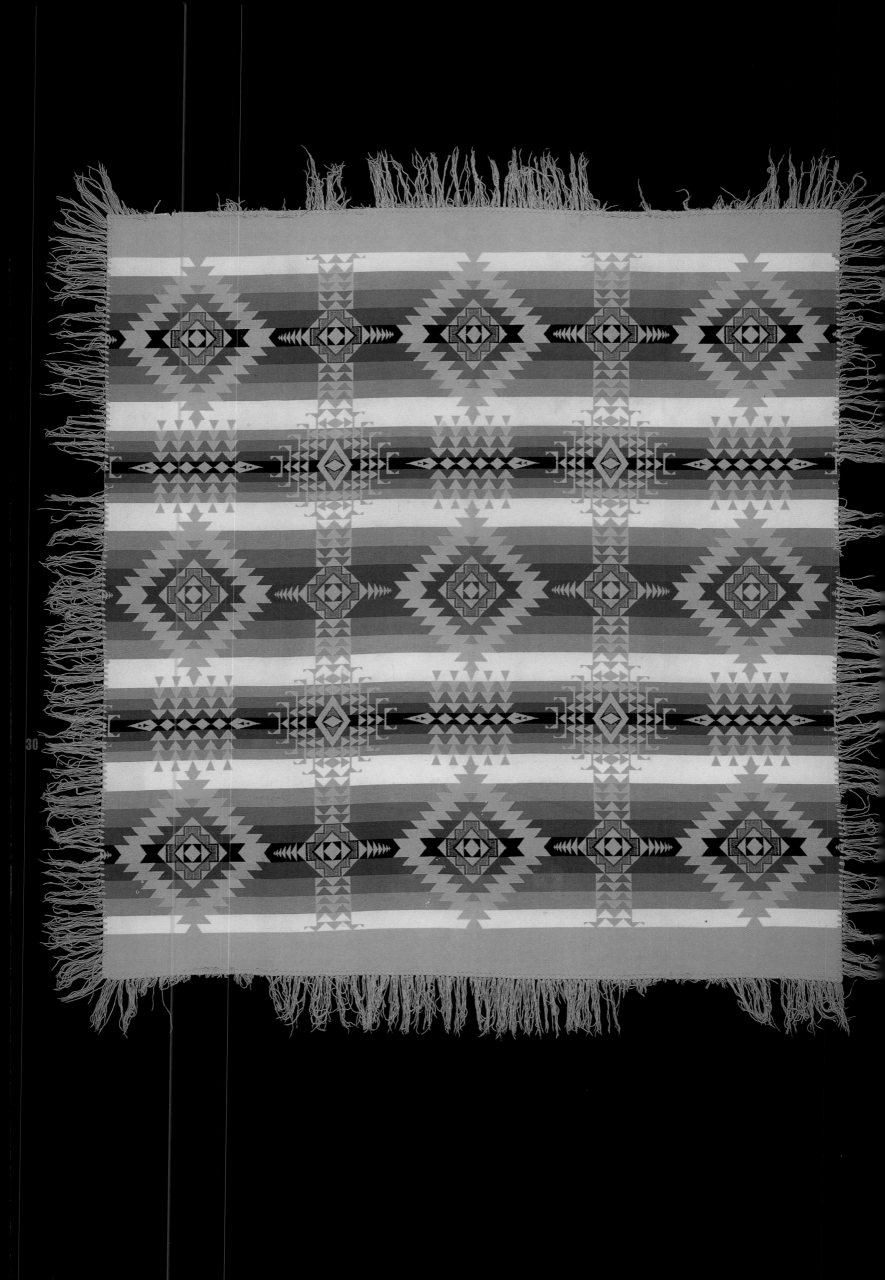

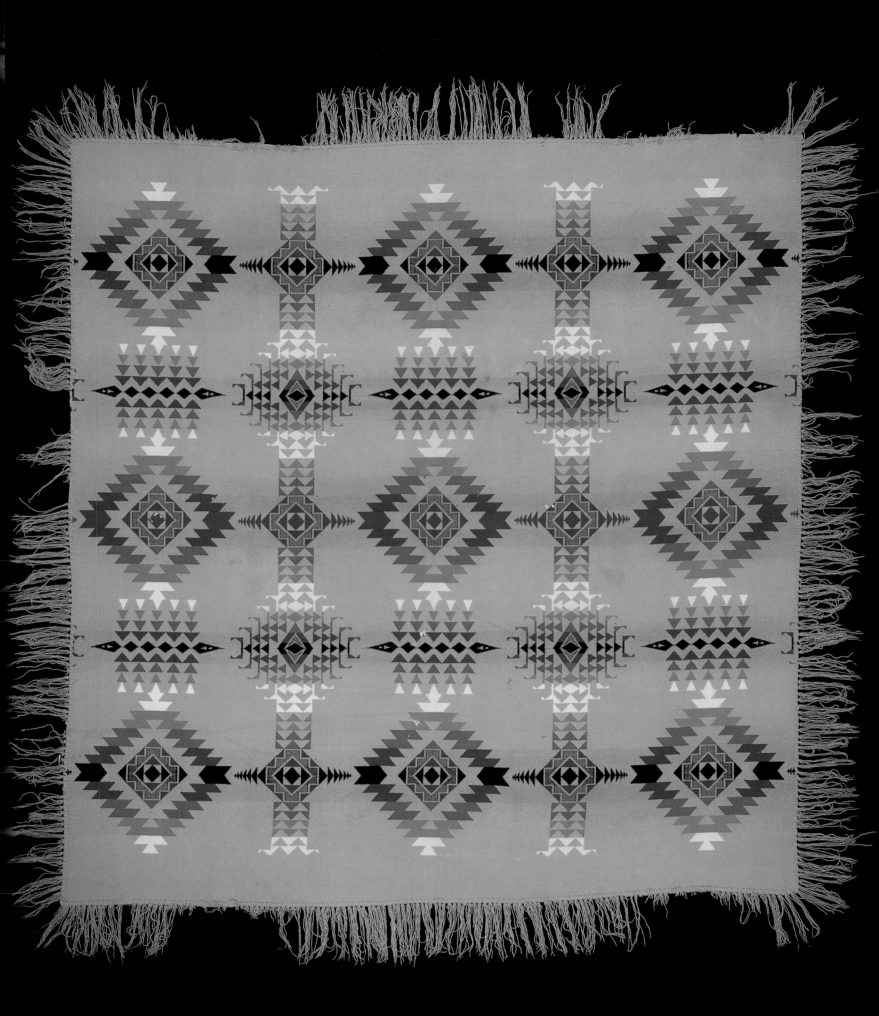

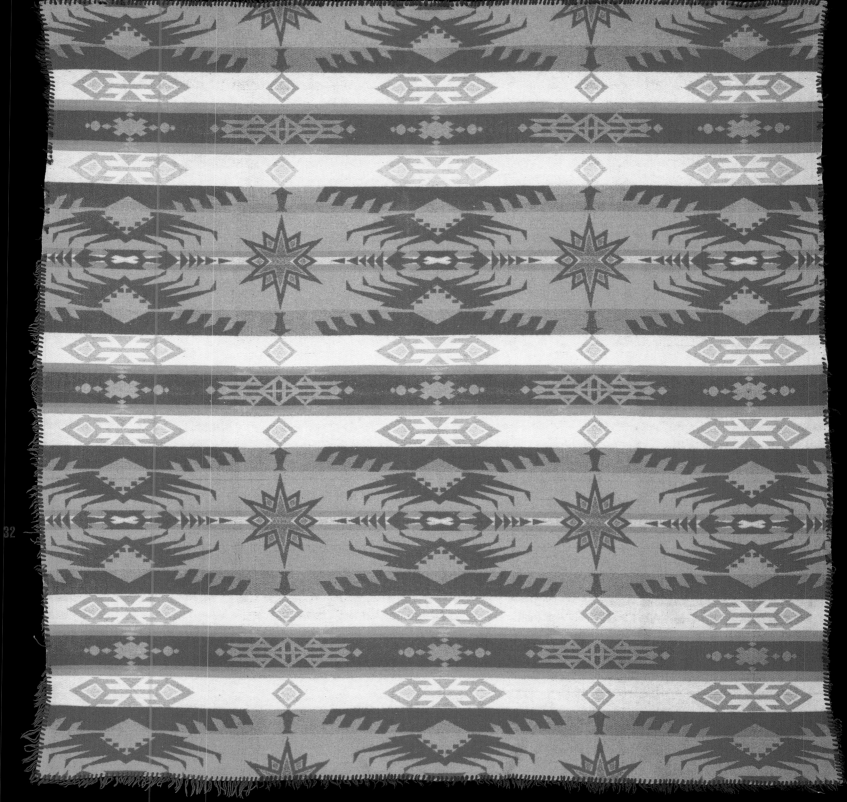

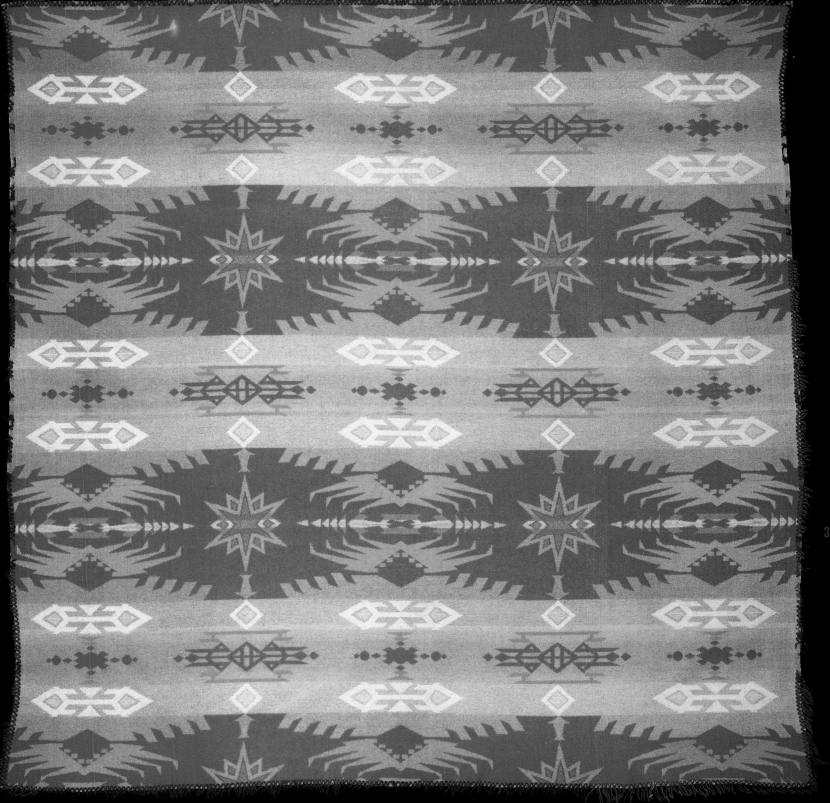

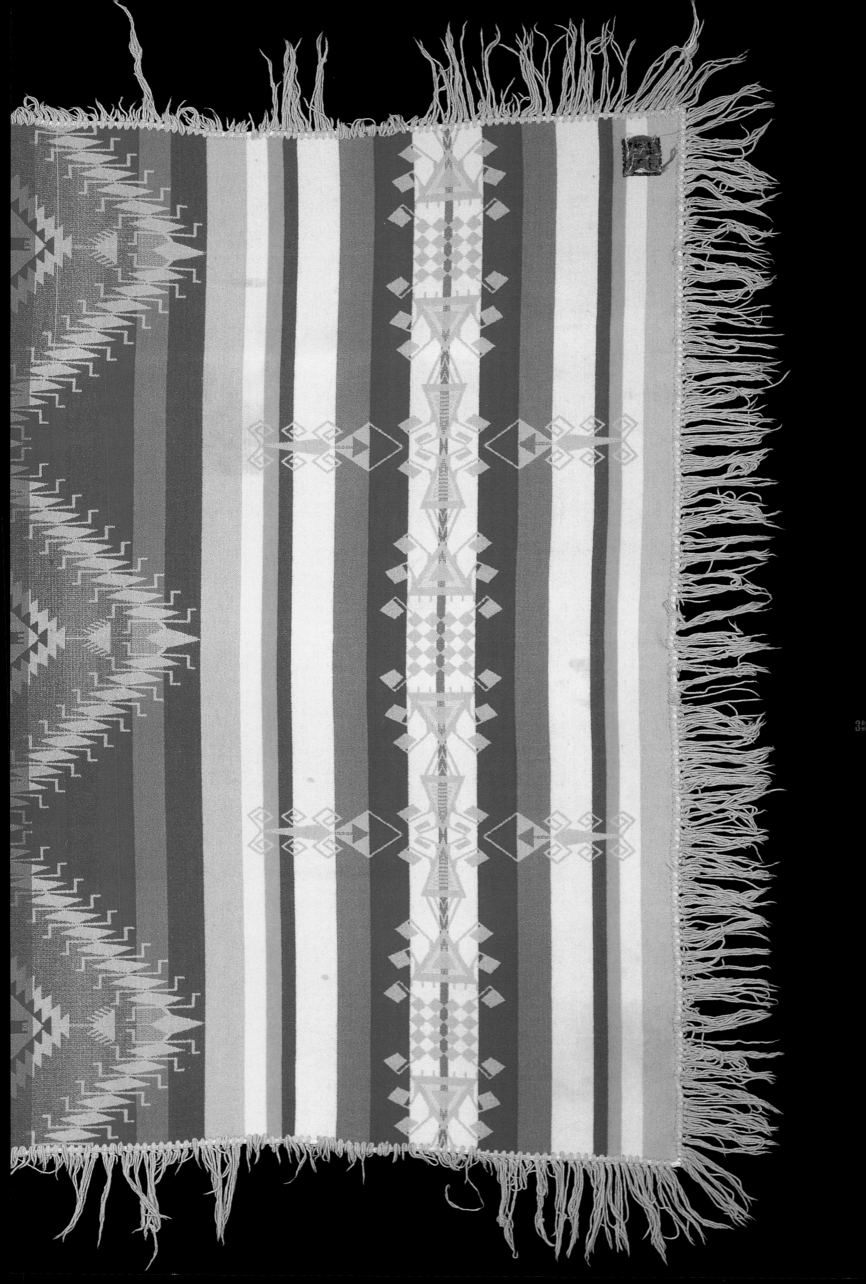

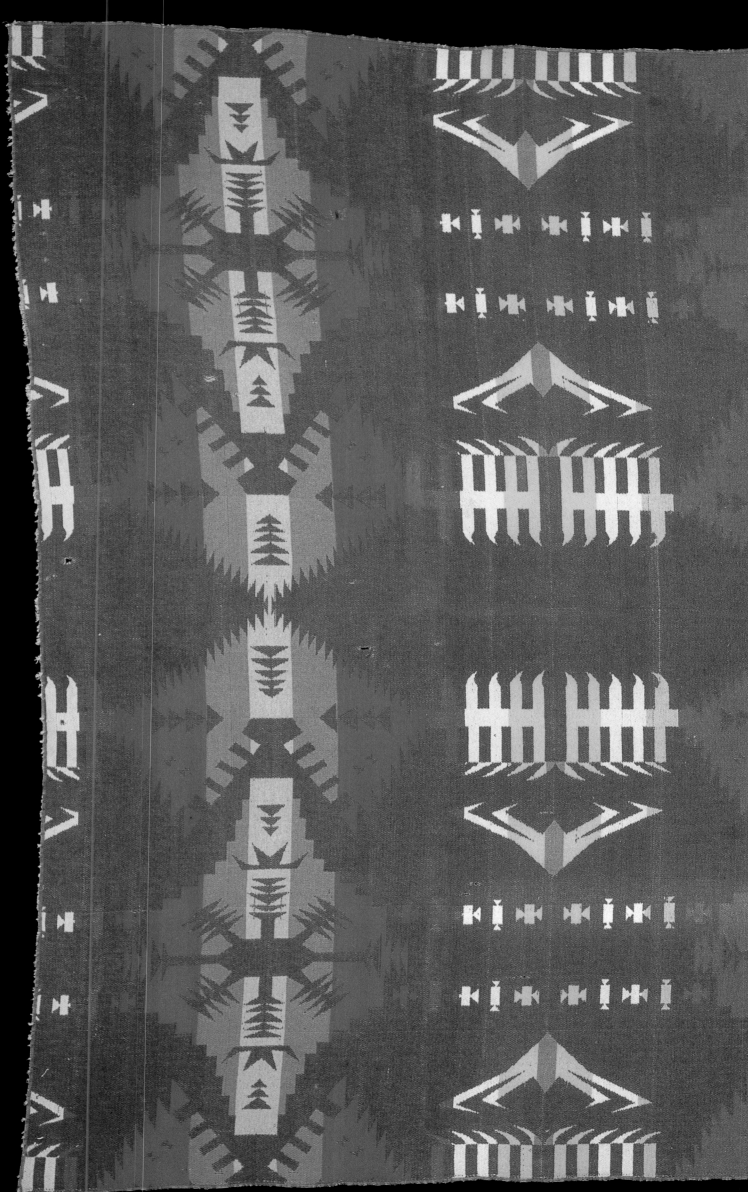

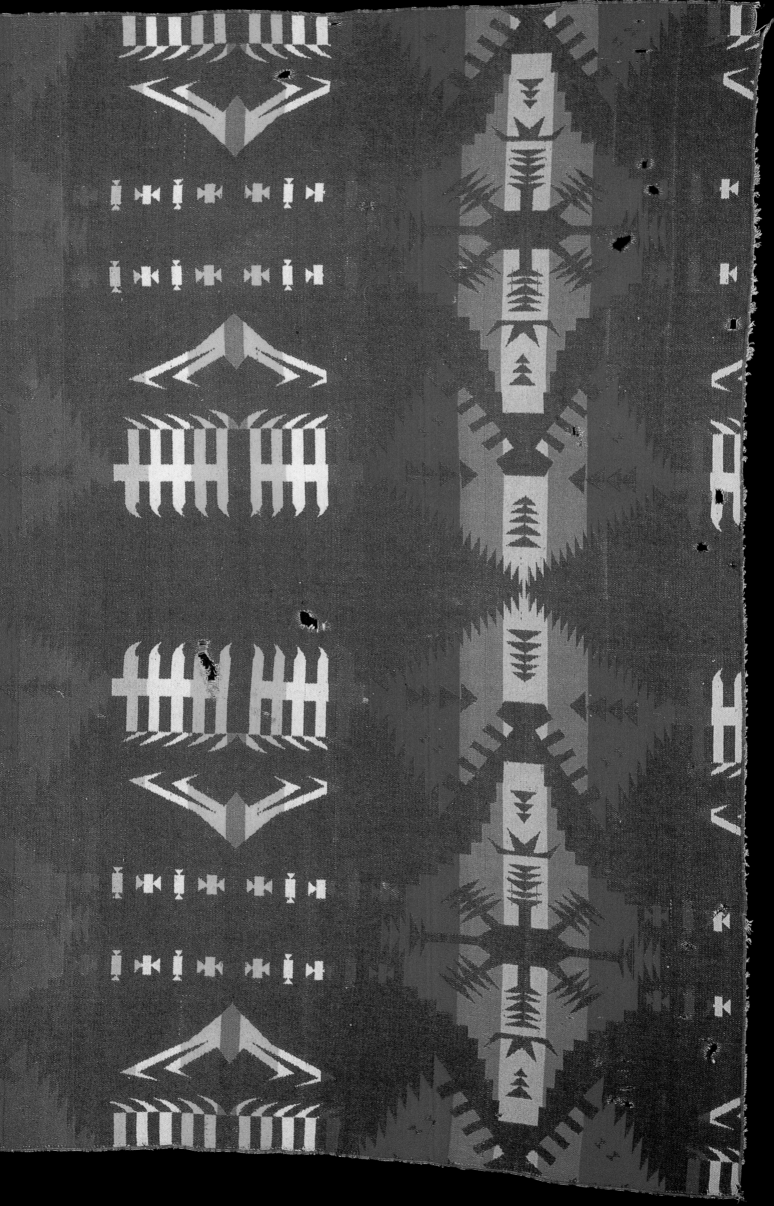

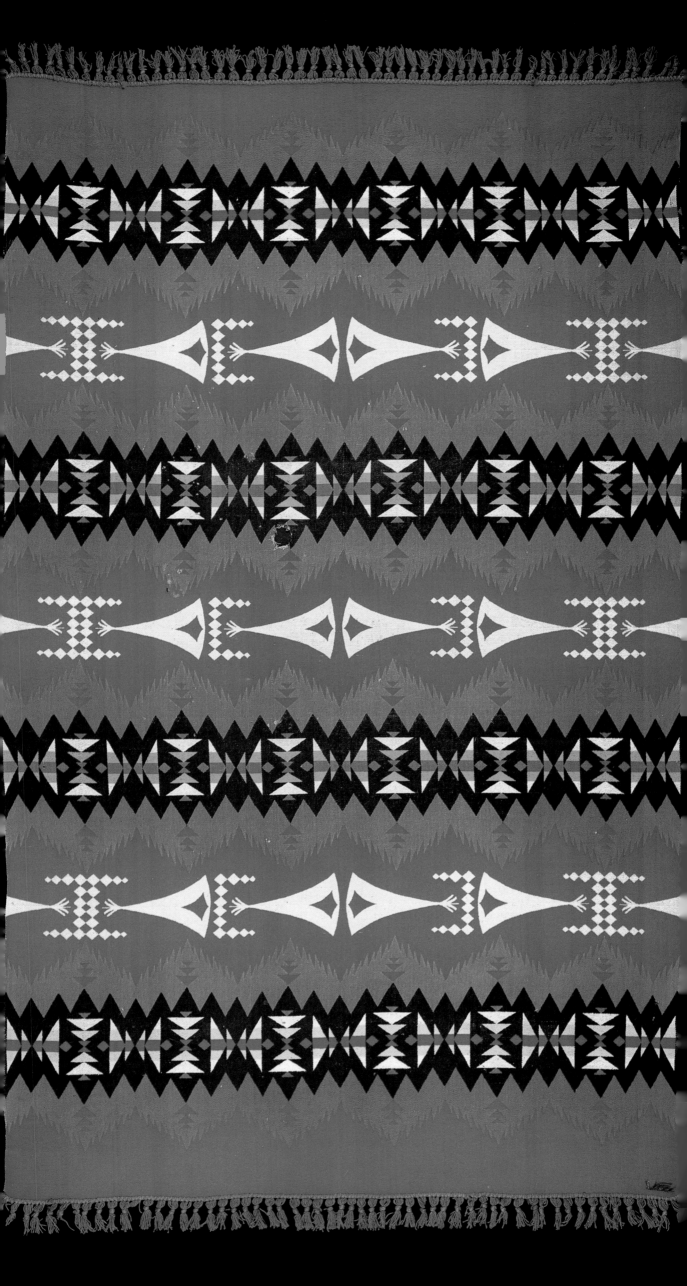

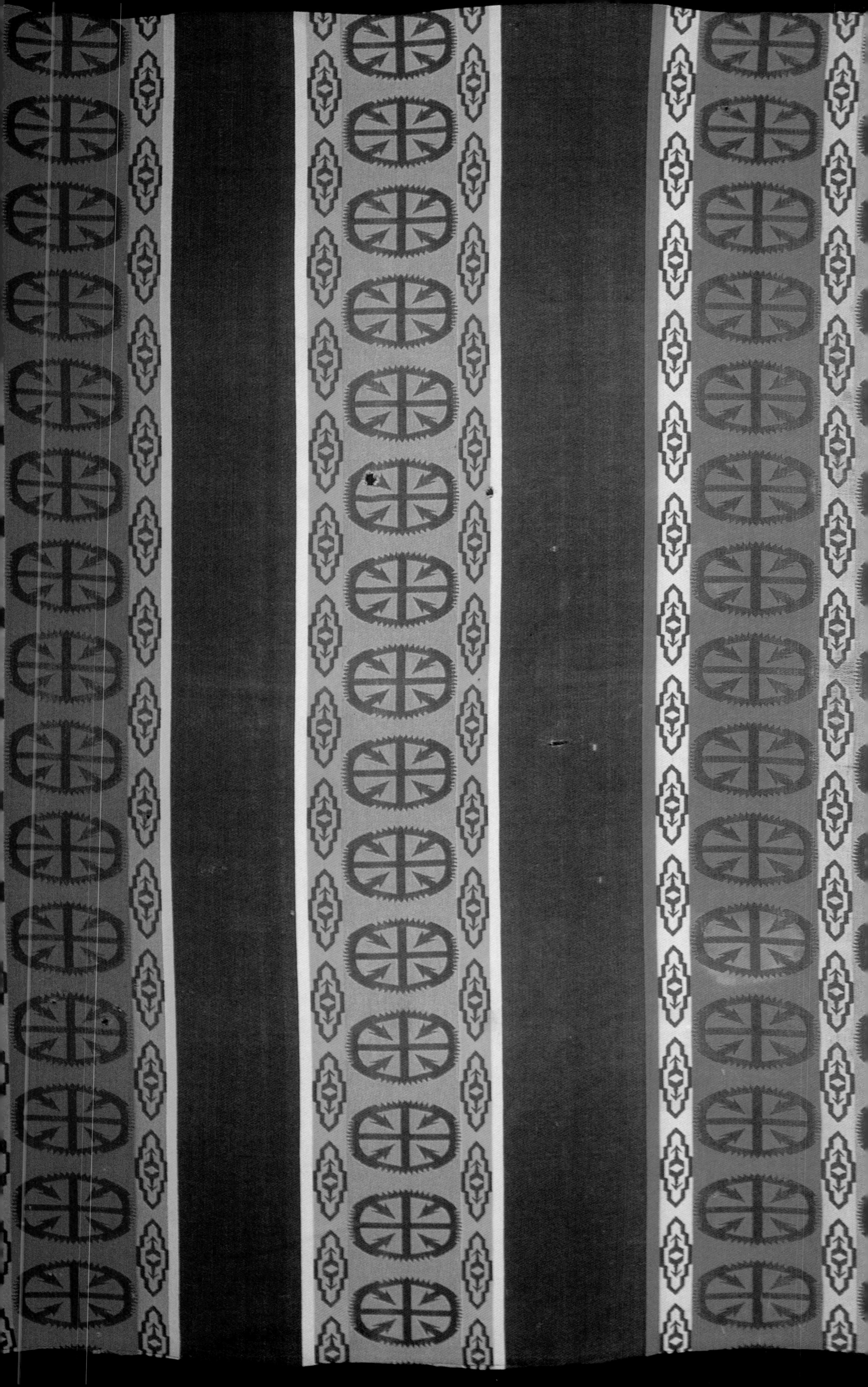

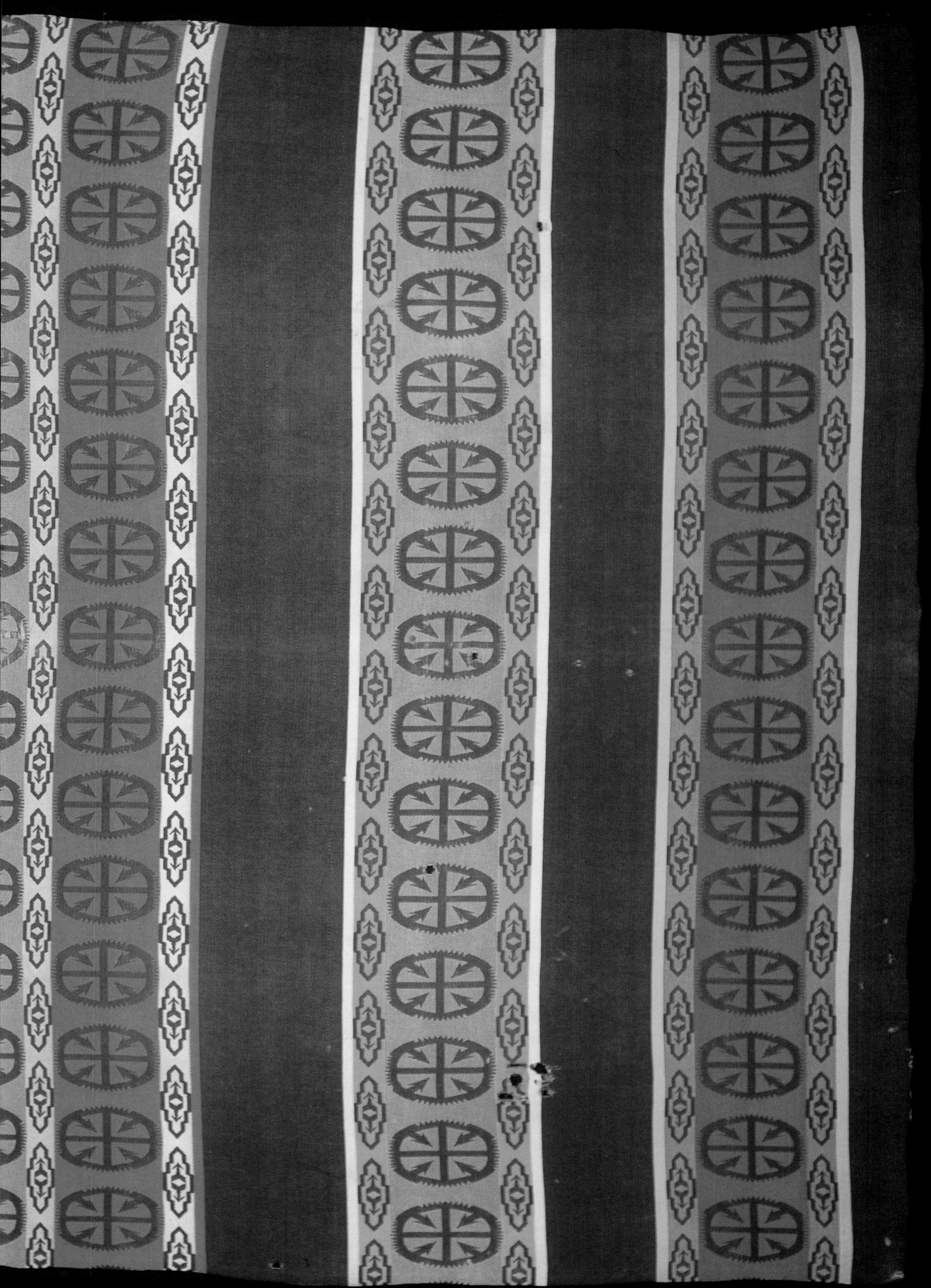

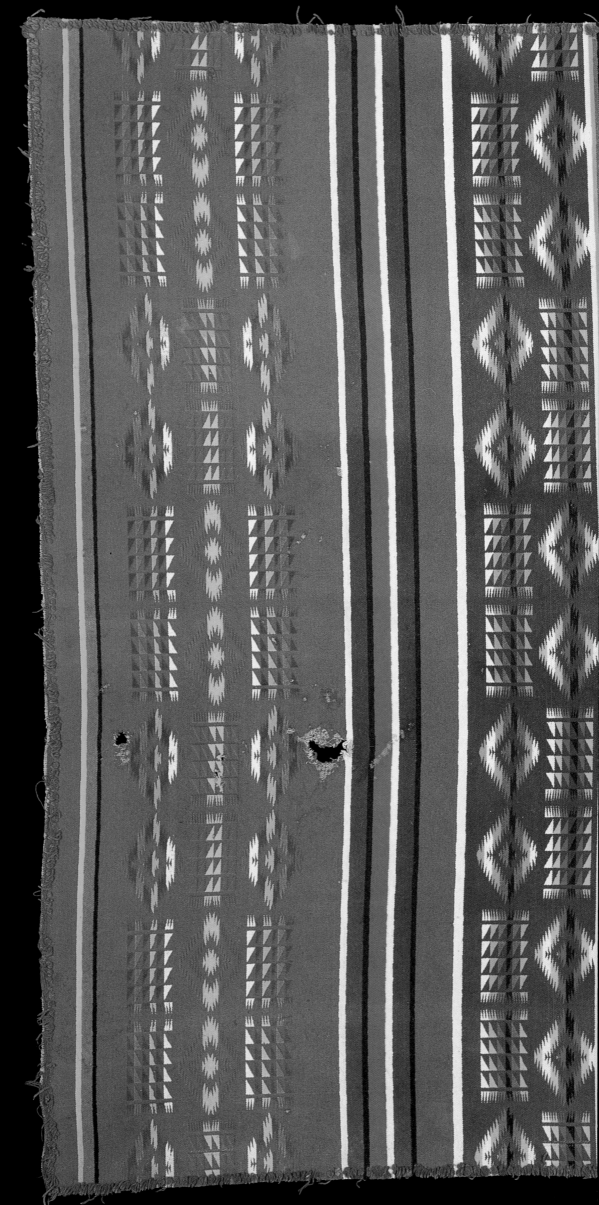

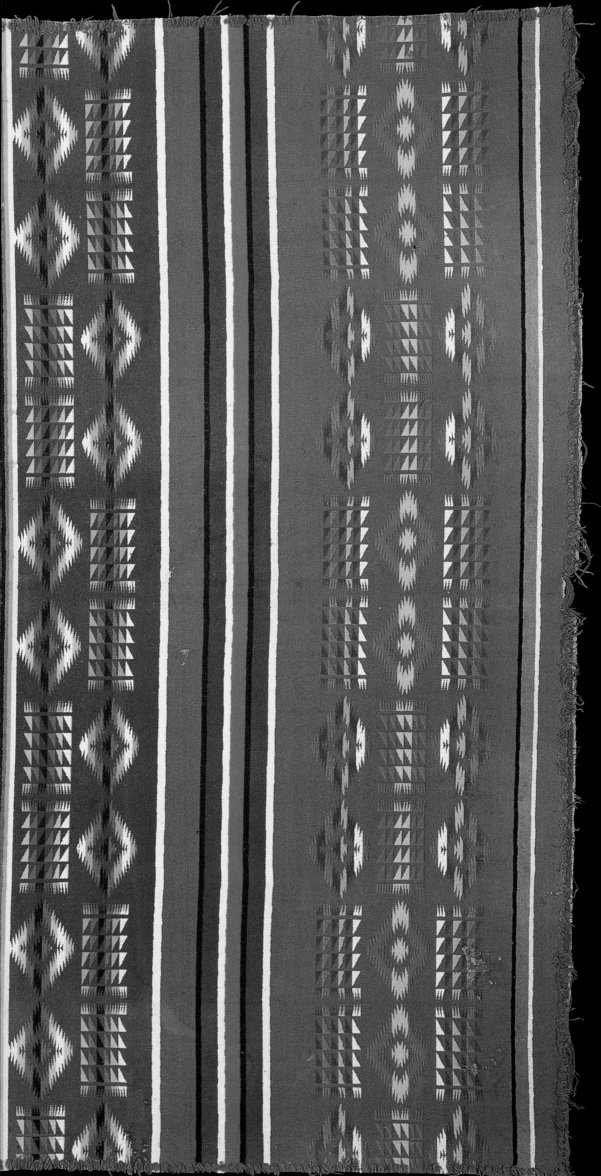

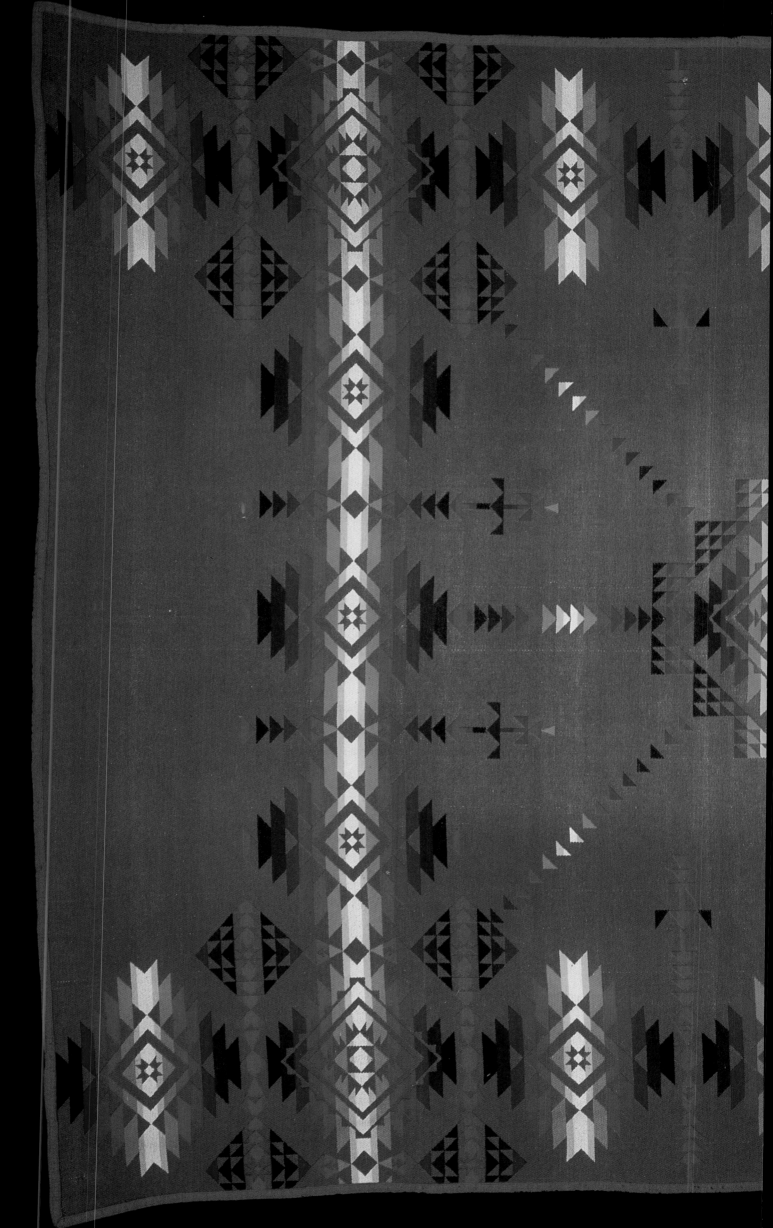

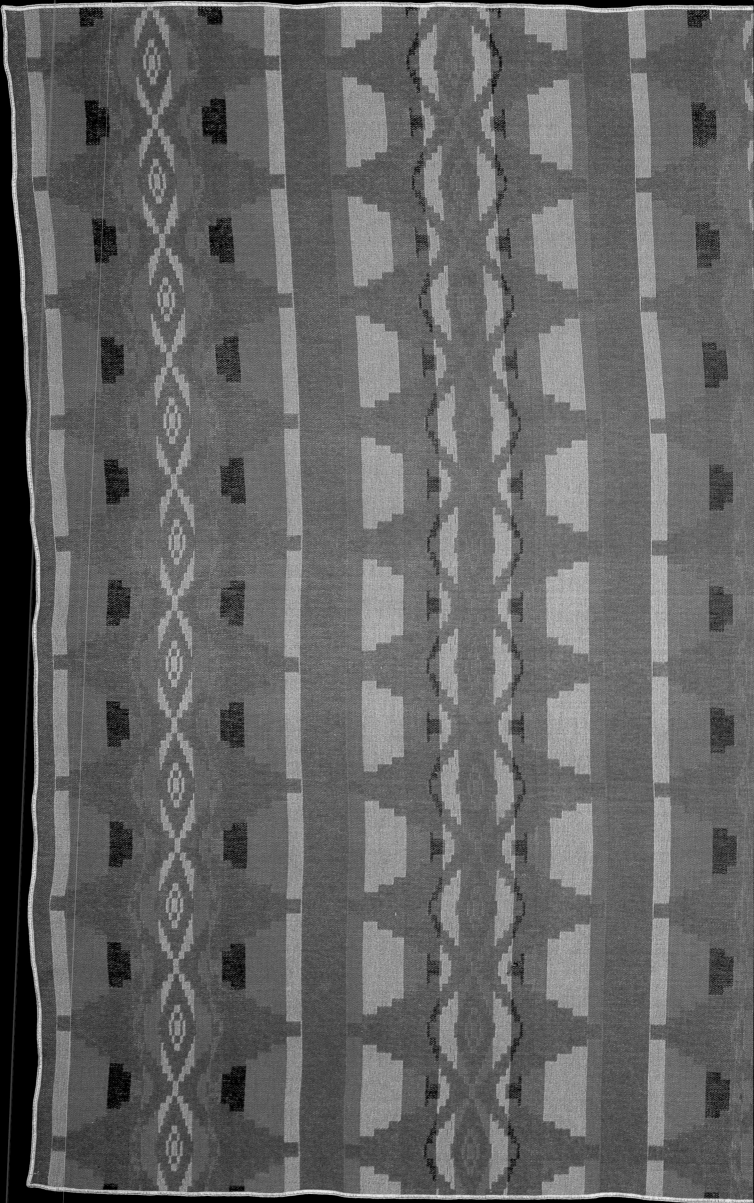

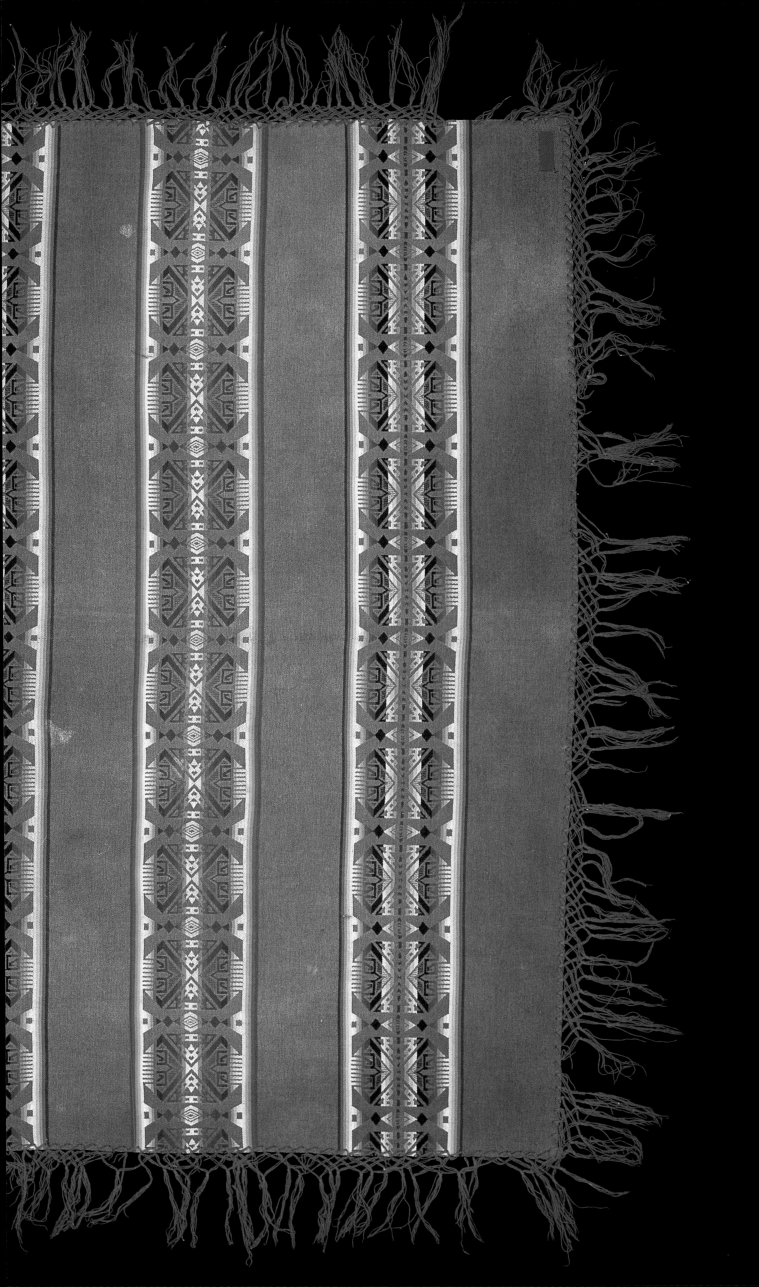

63

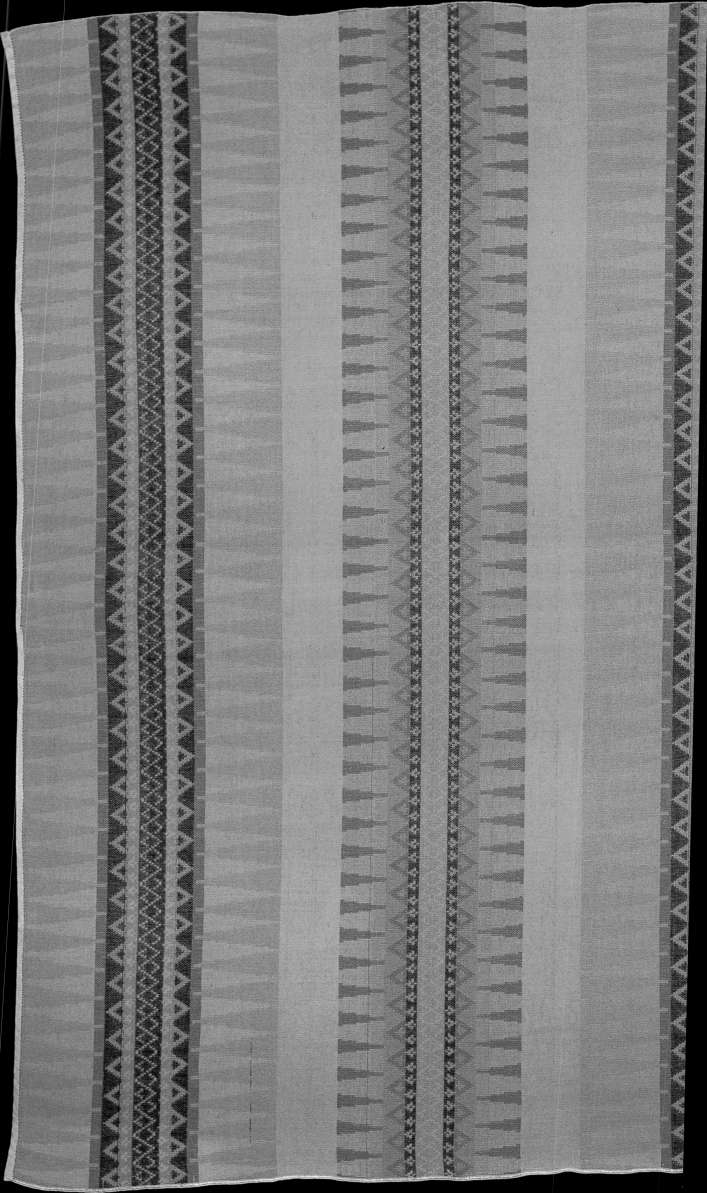

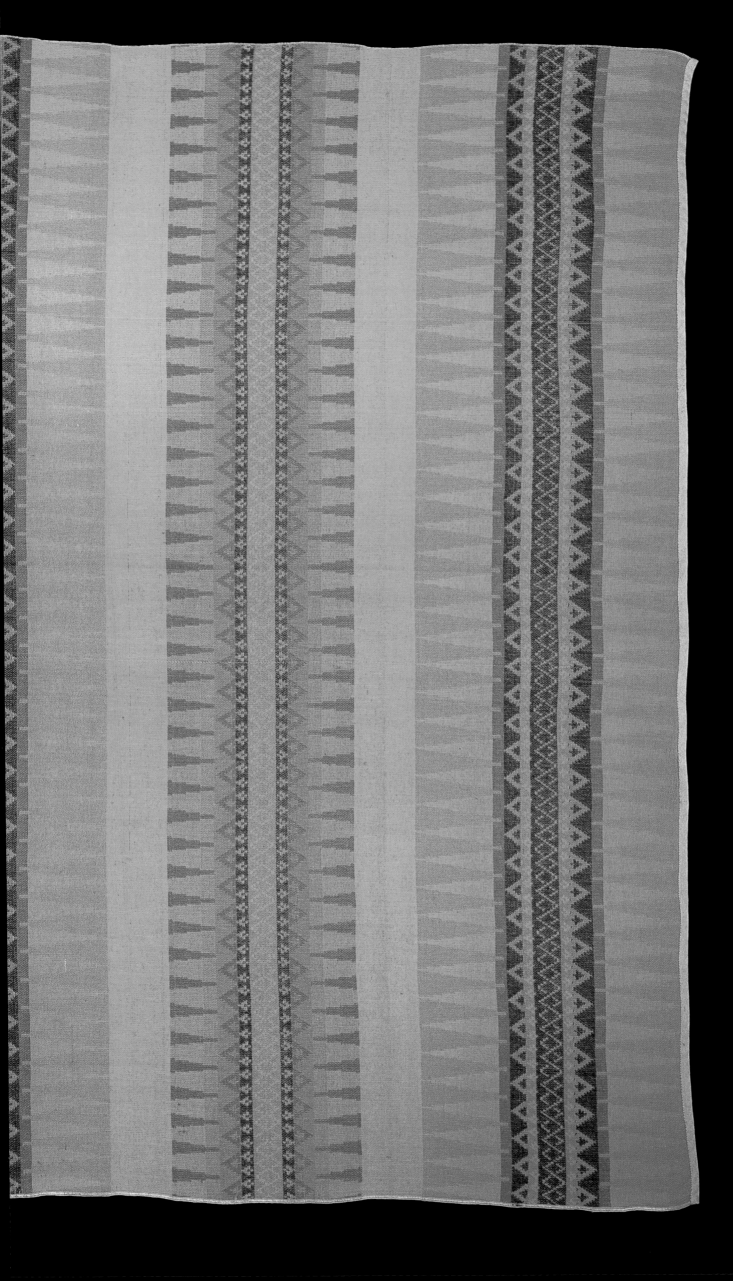

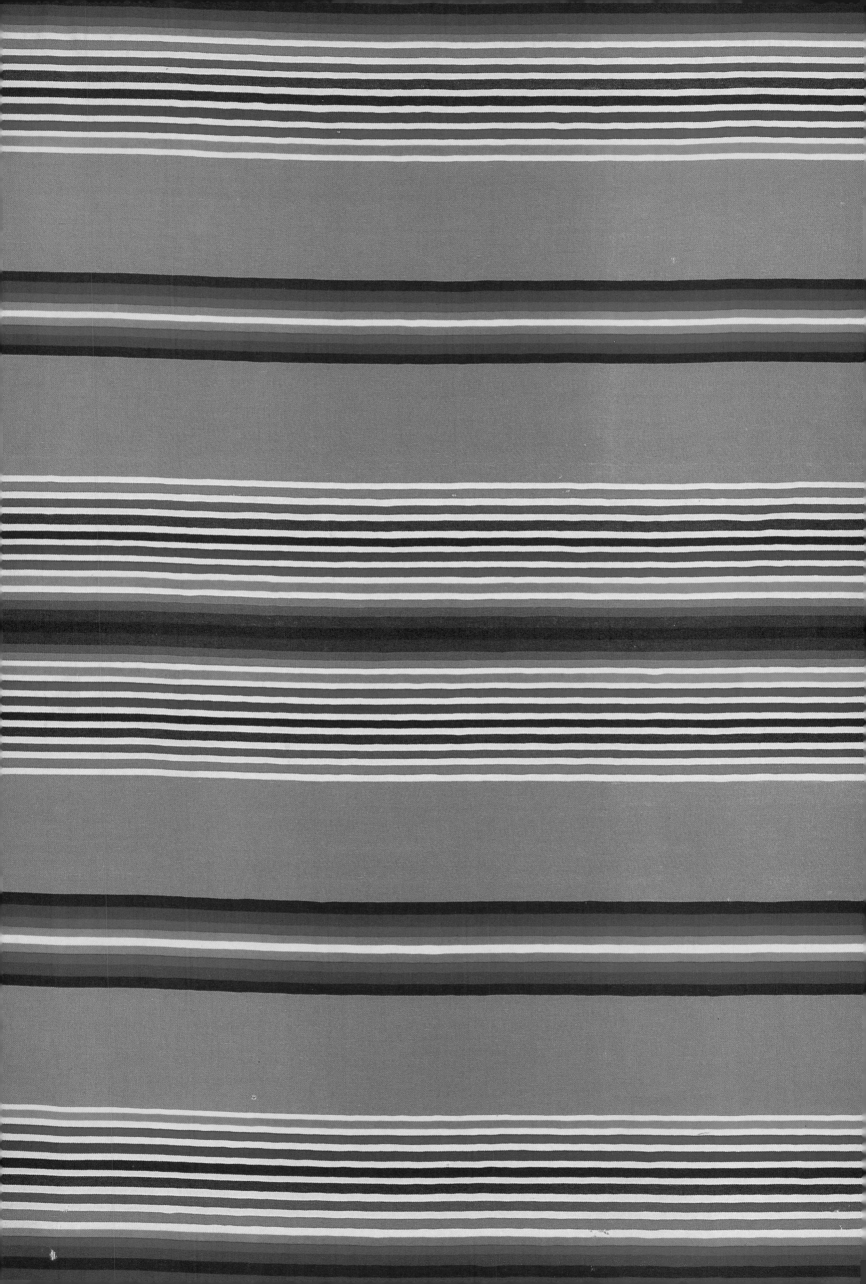

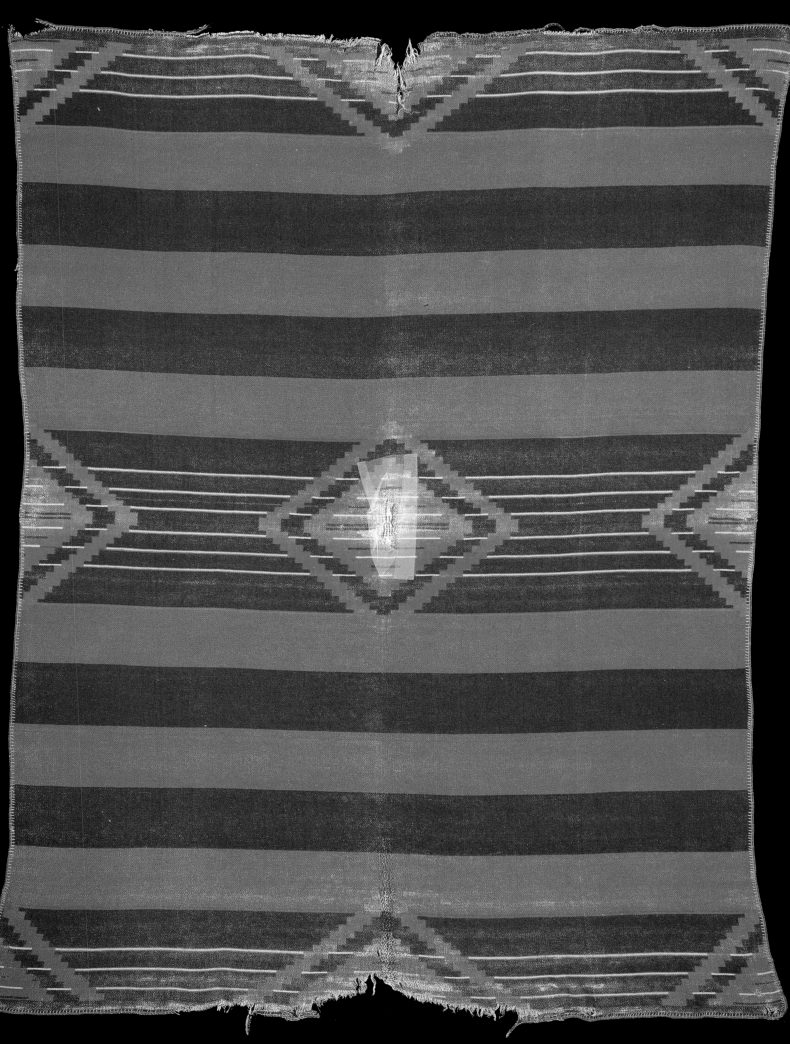

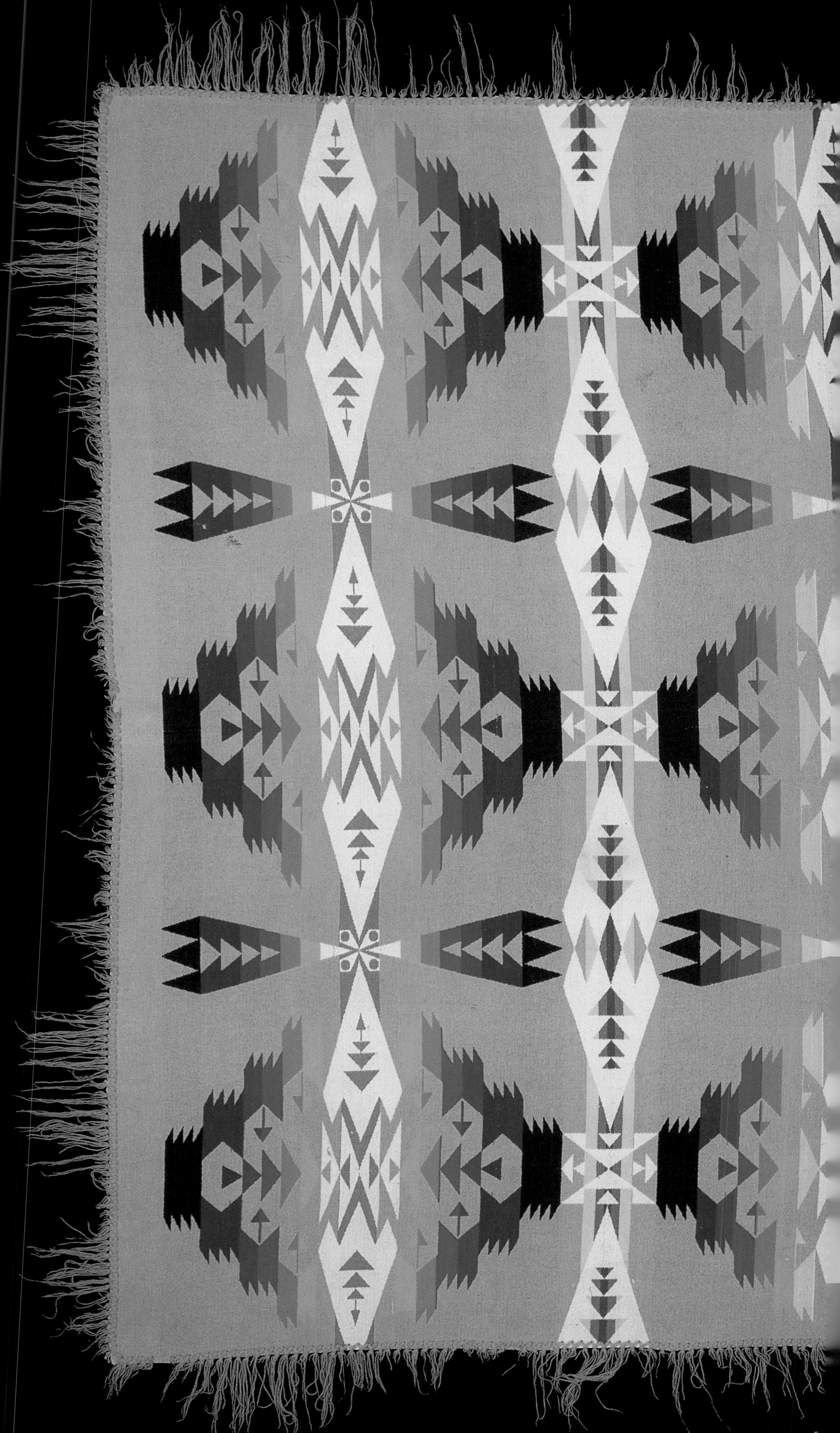

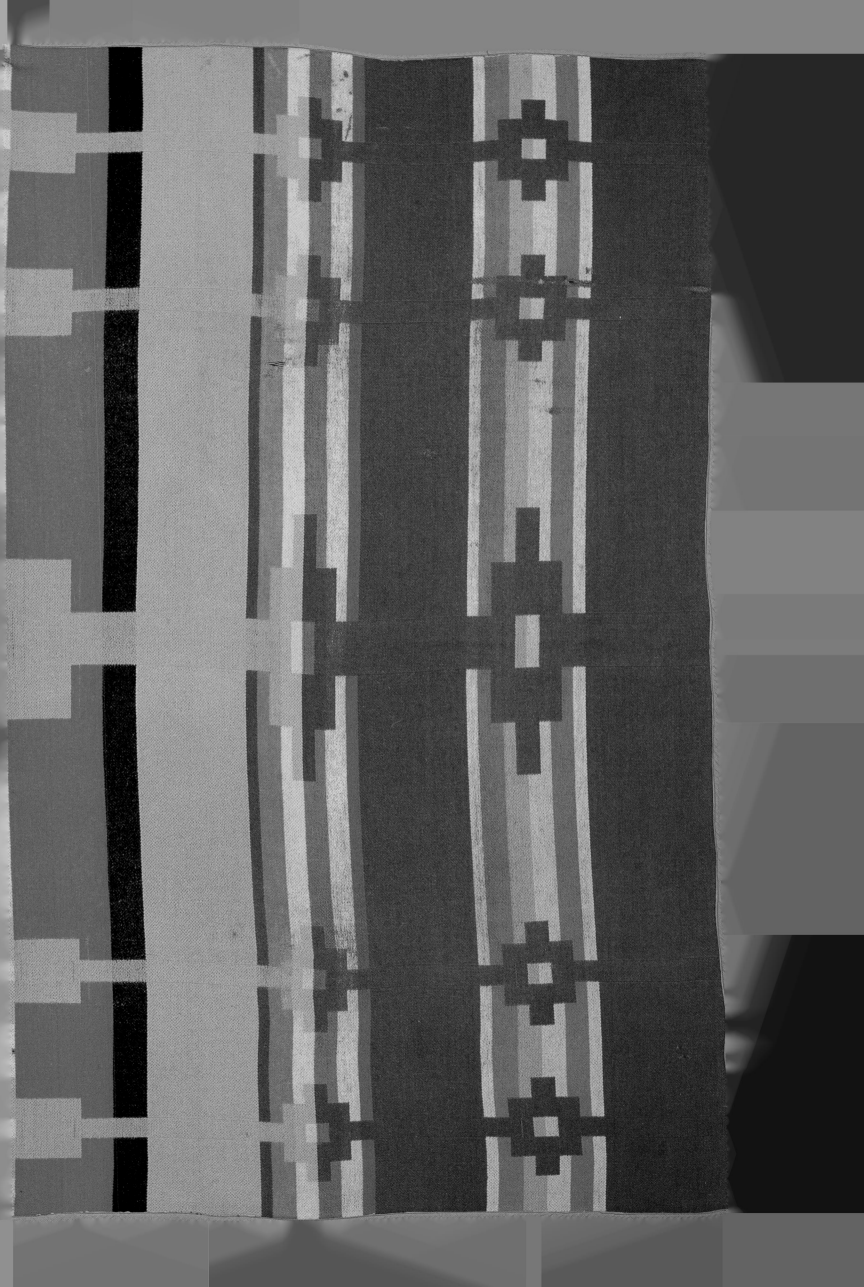

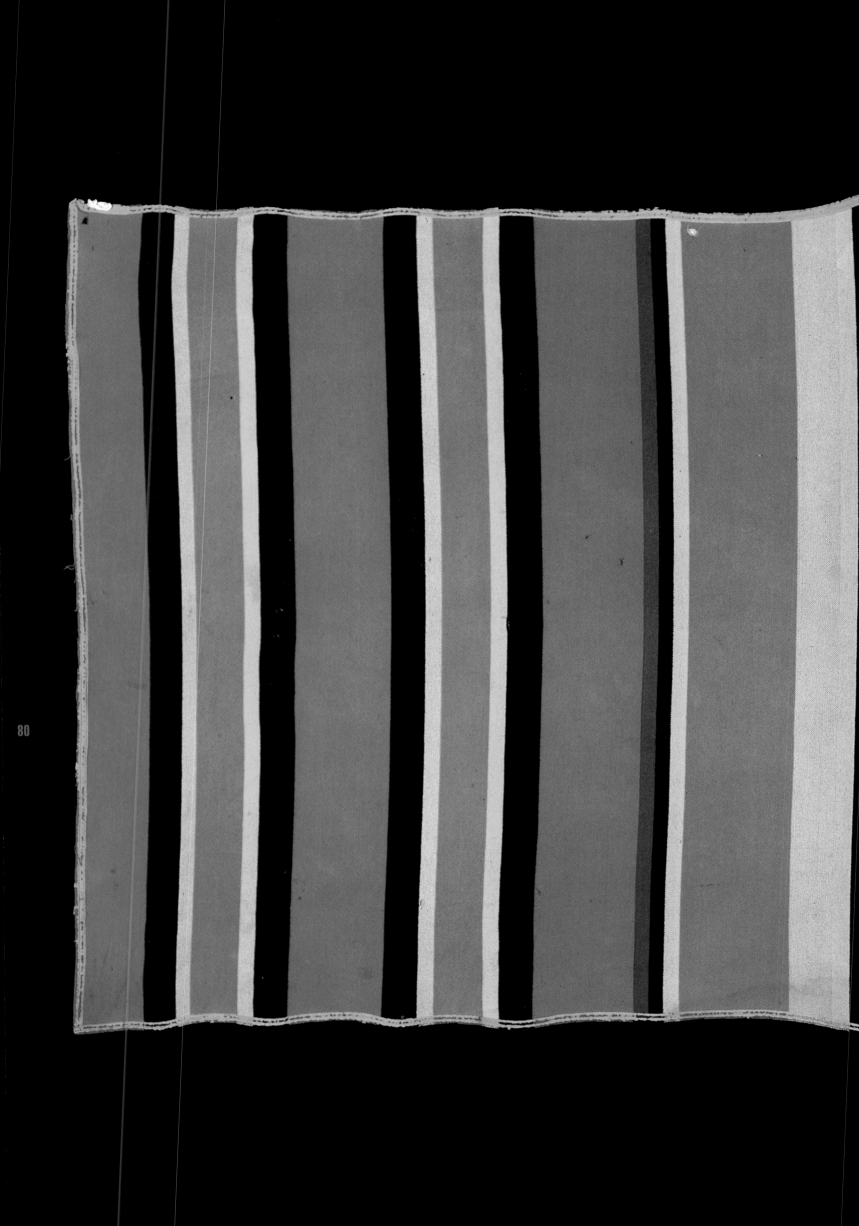

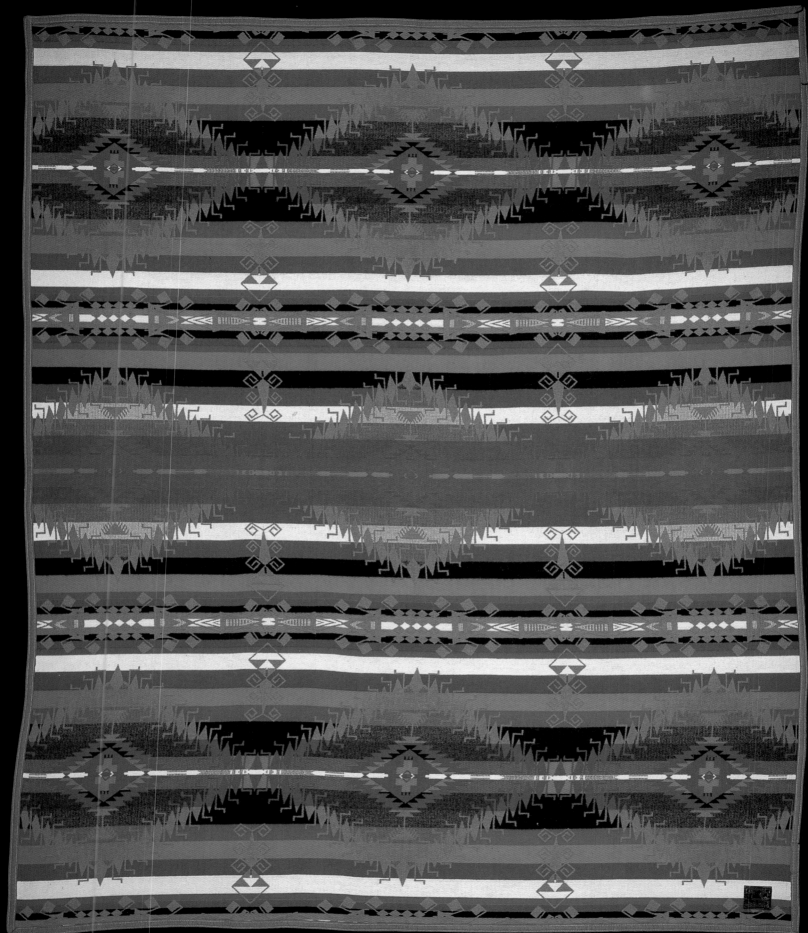

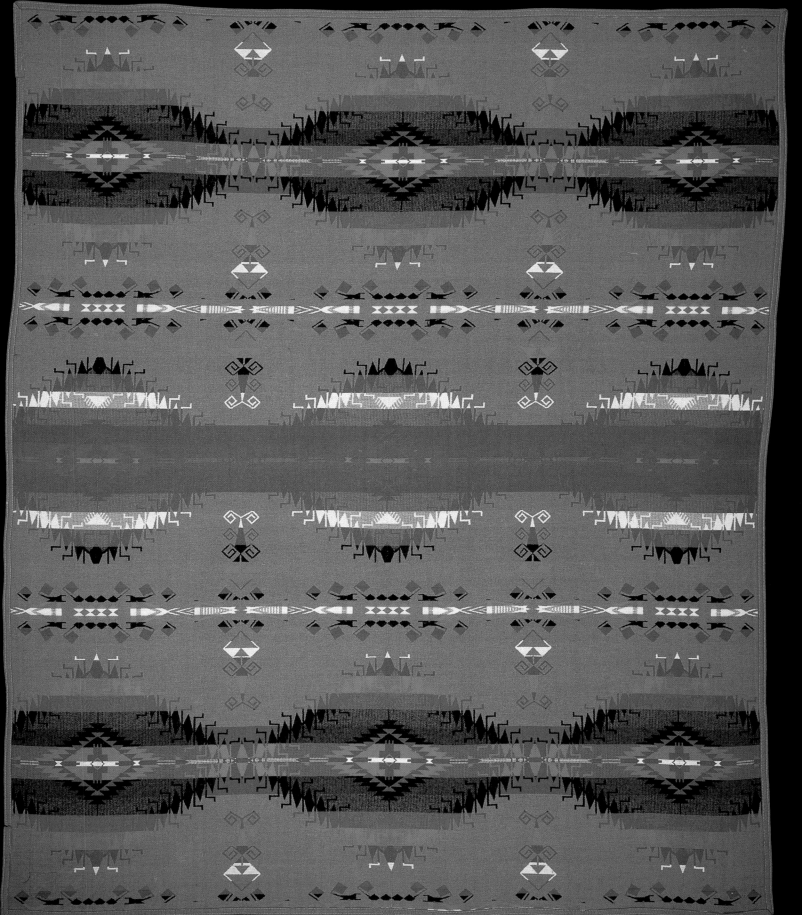

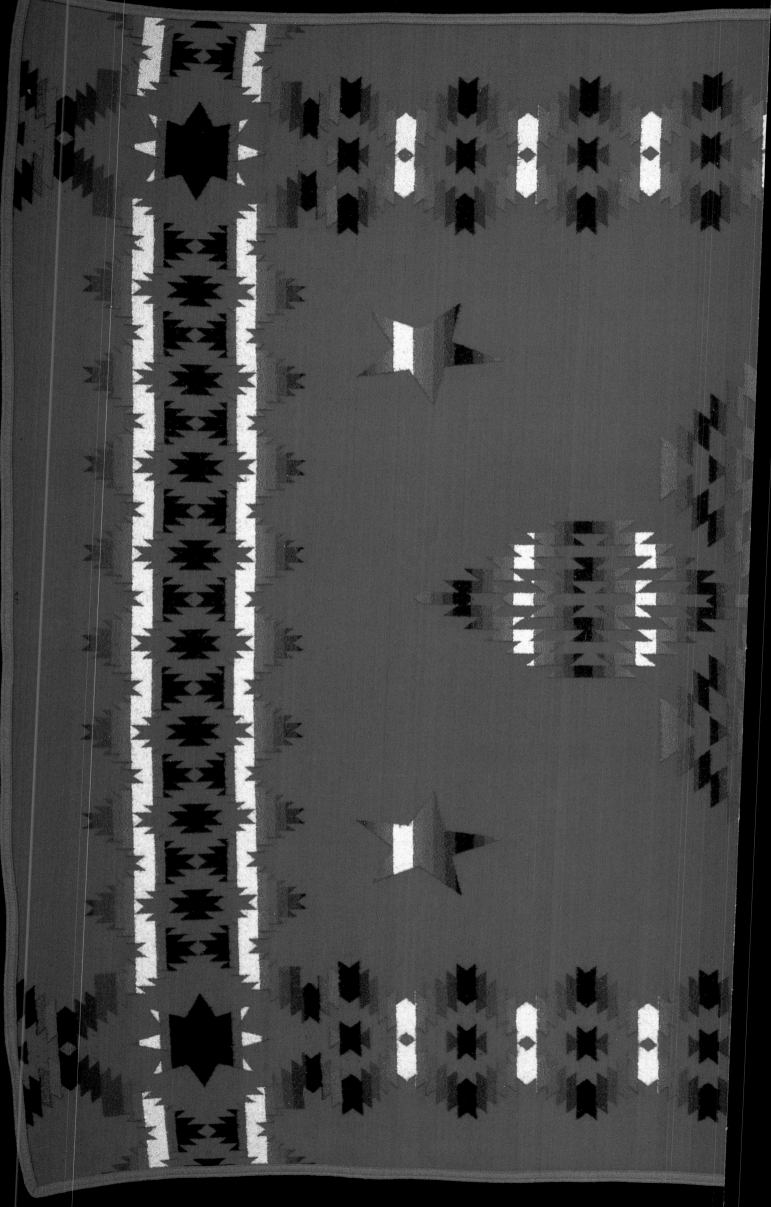

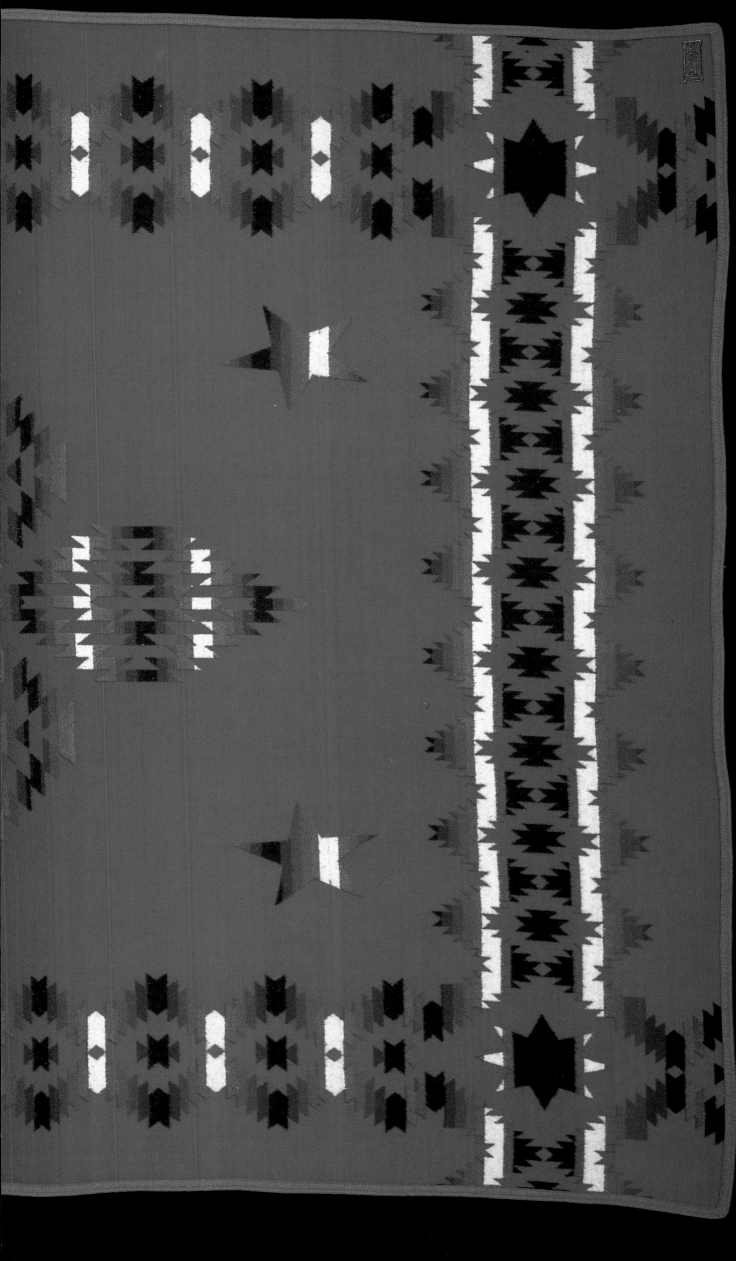

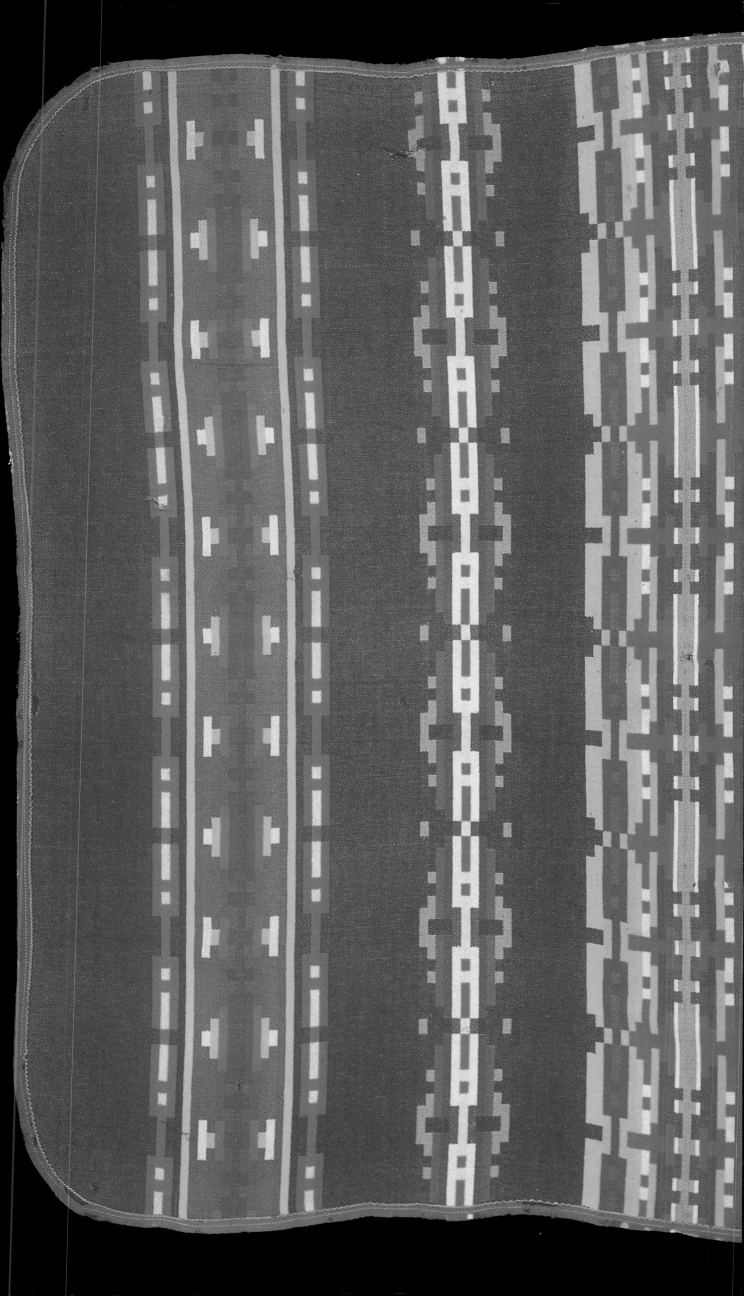

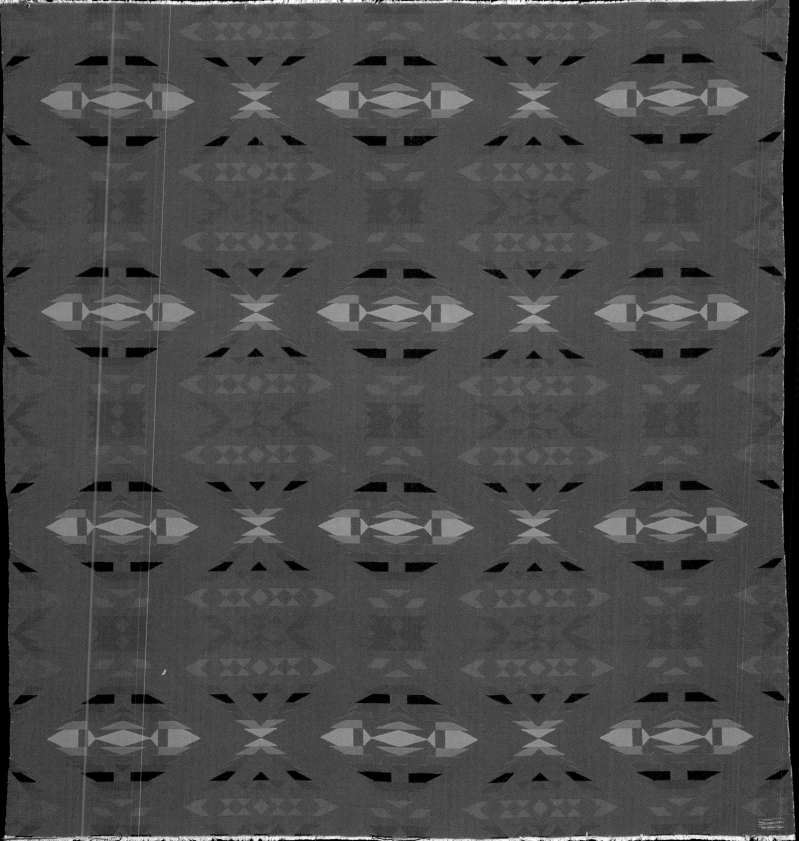

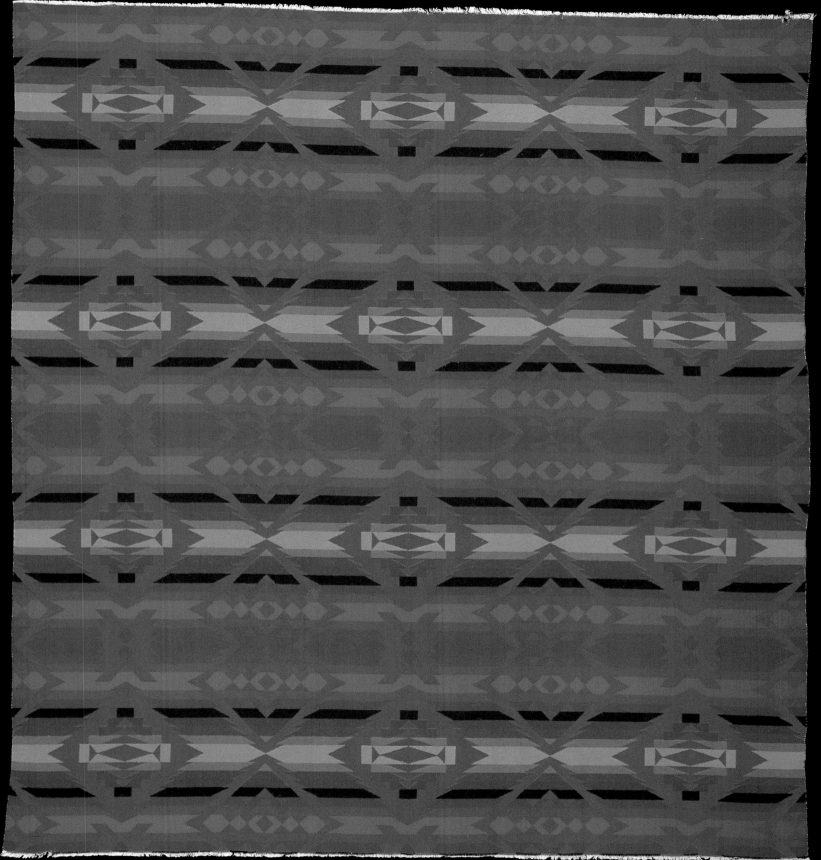

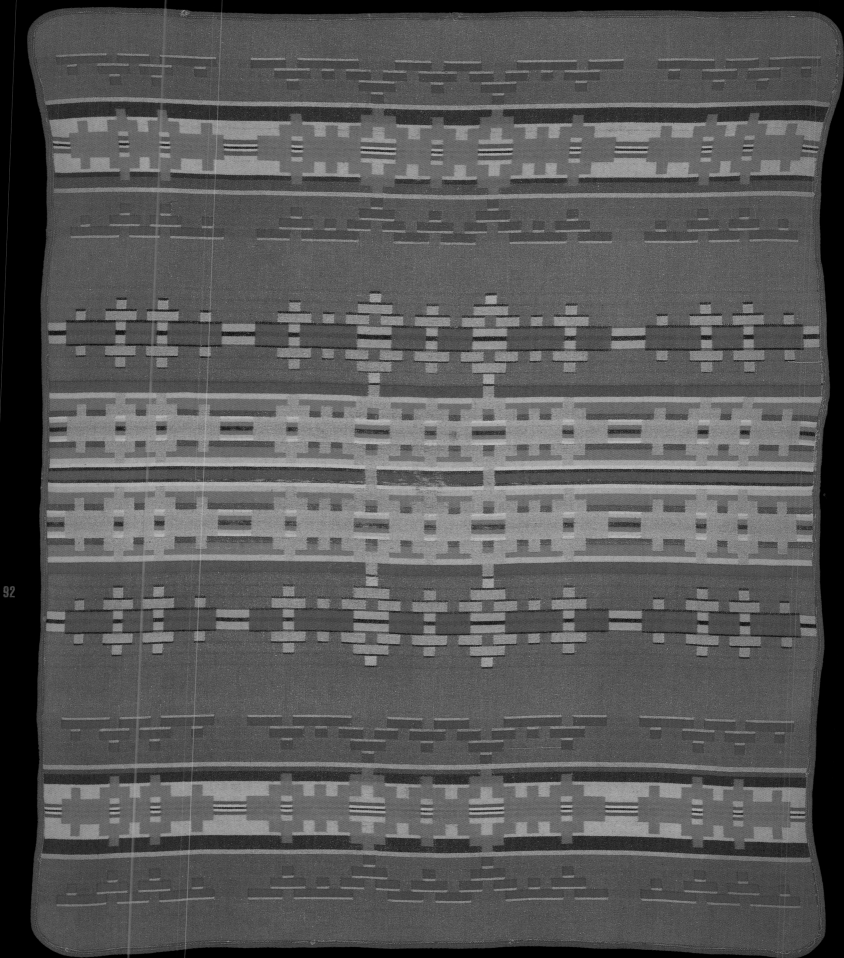

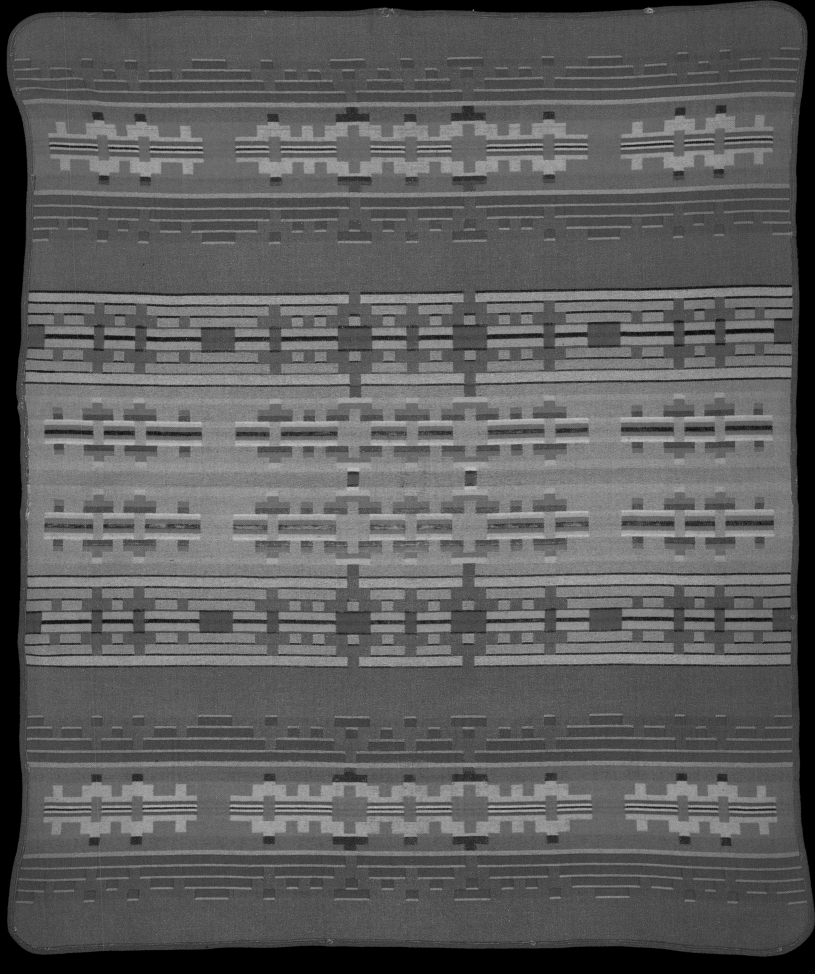

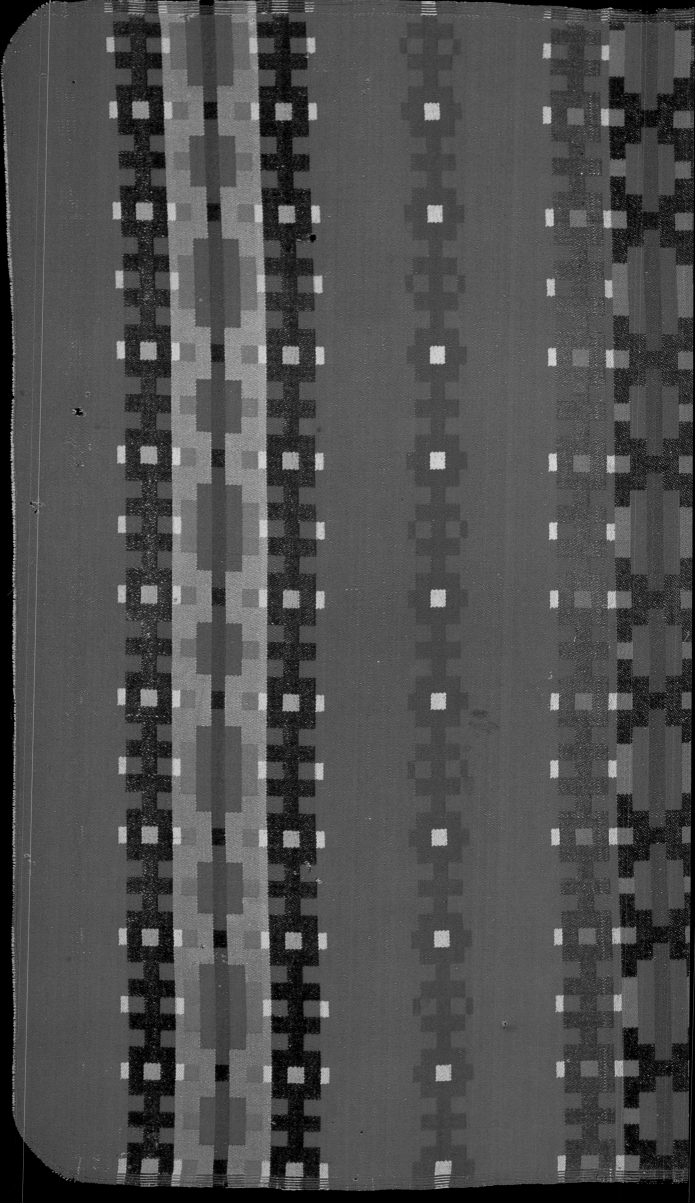

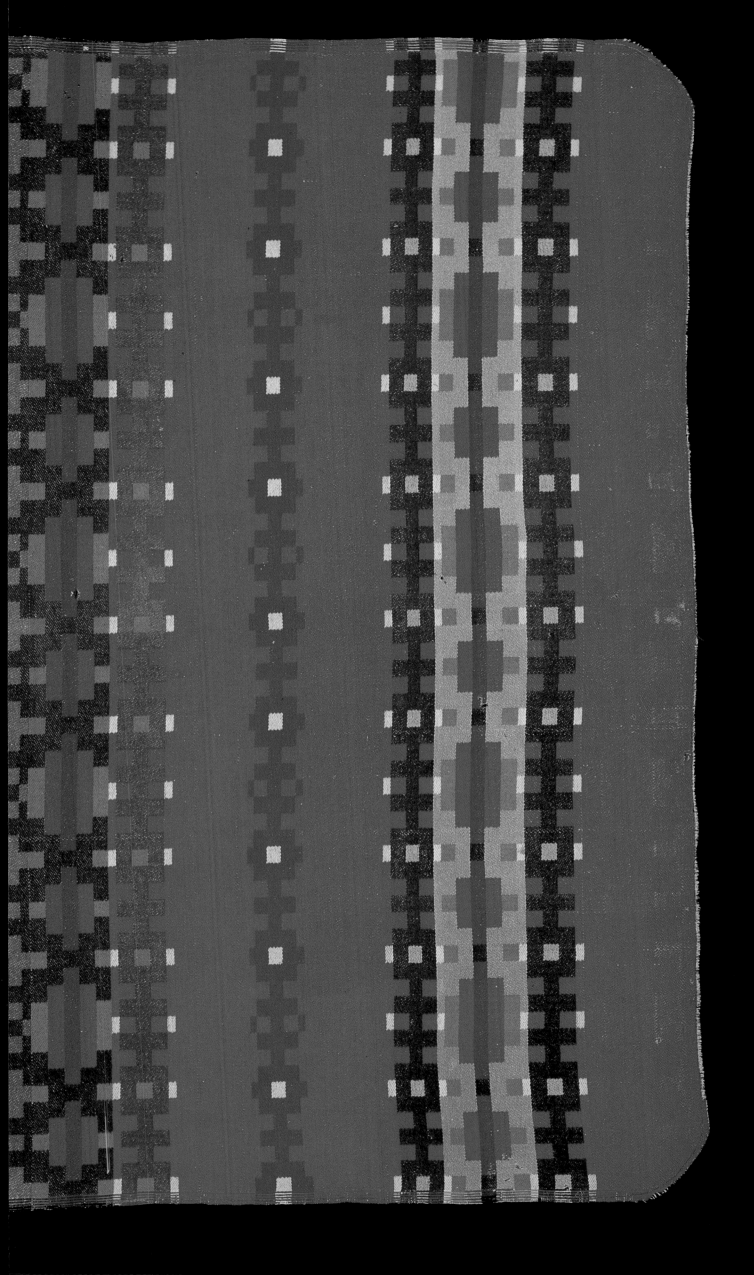

96

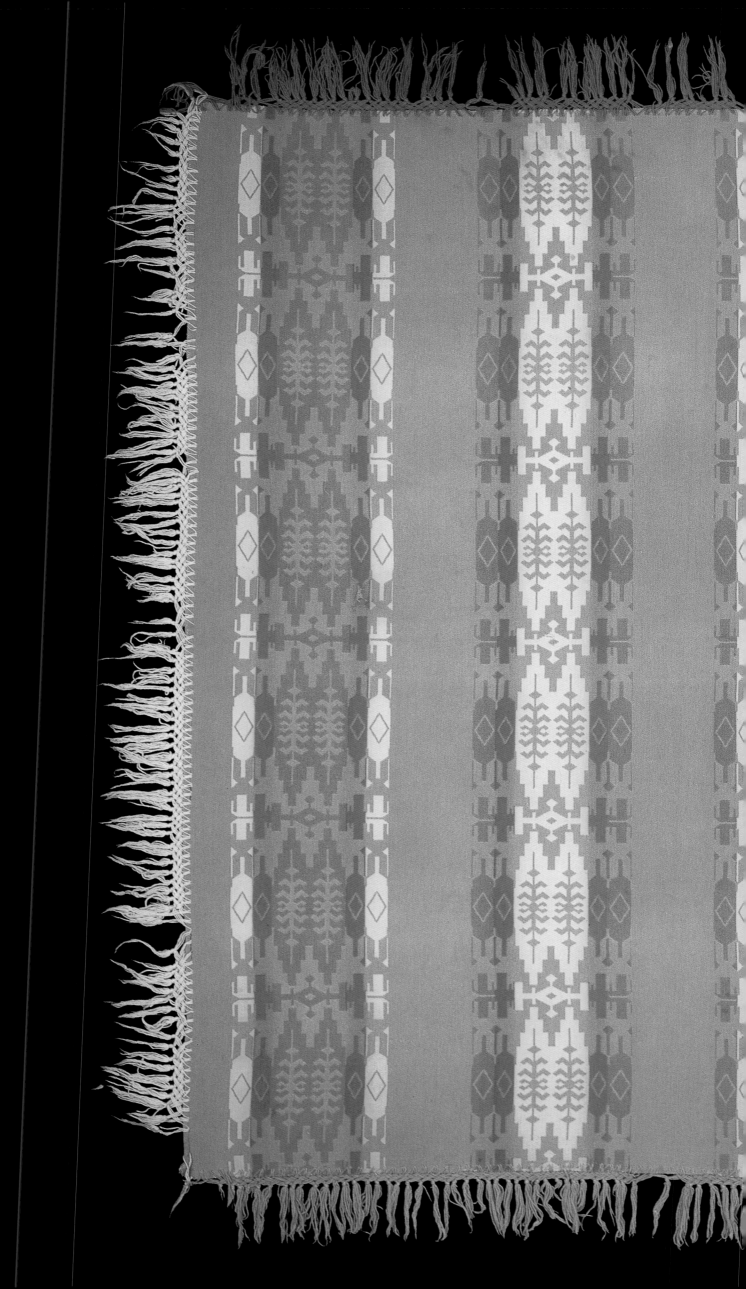

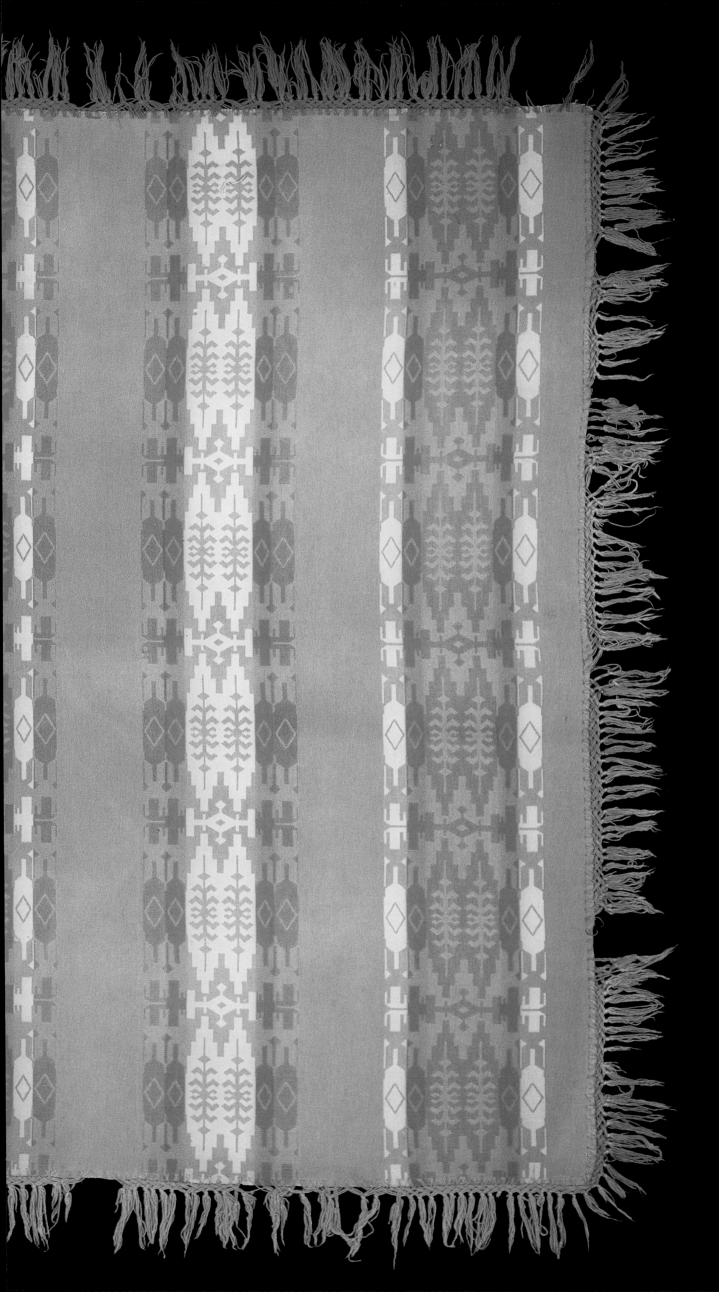

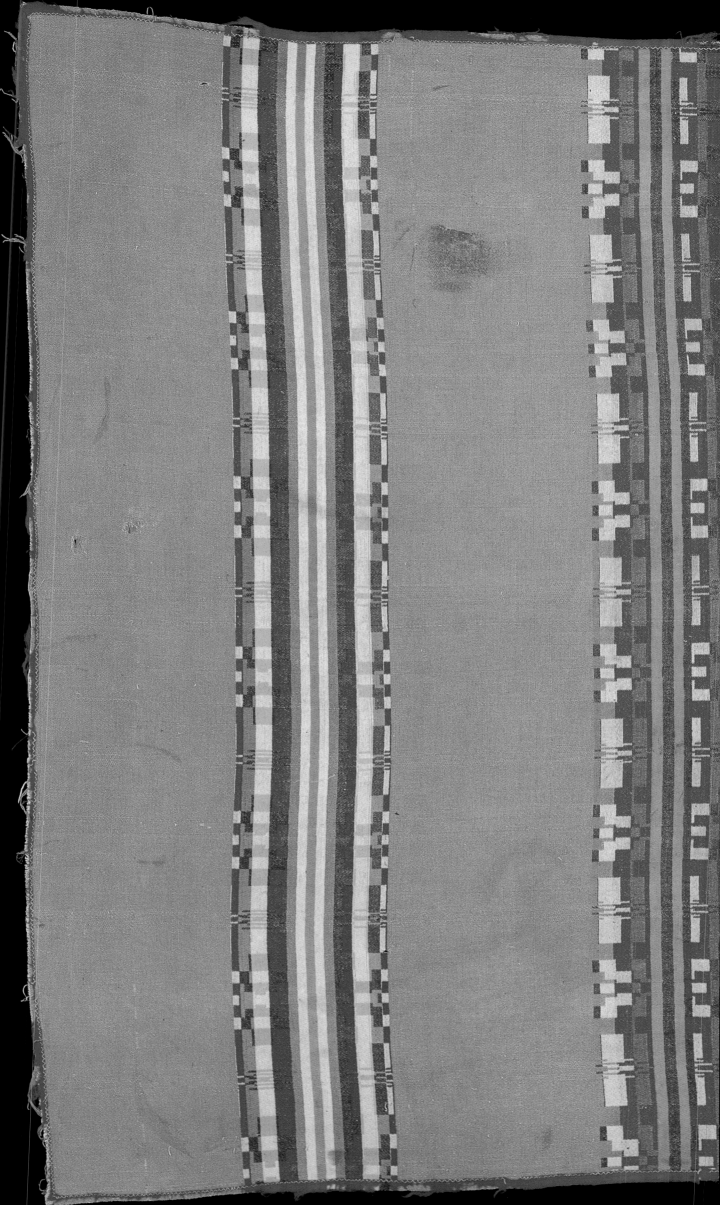

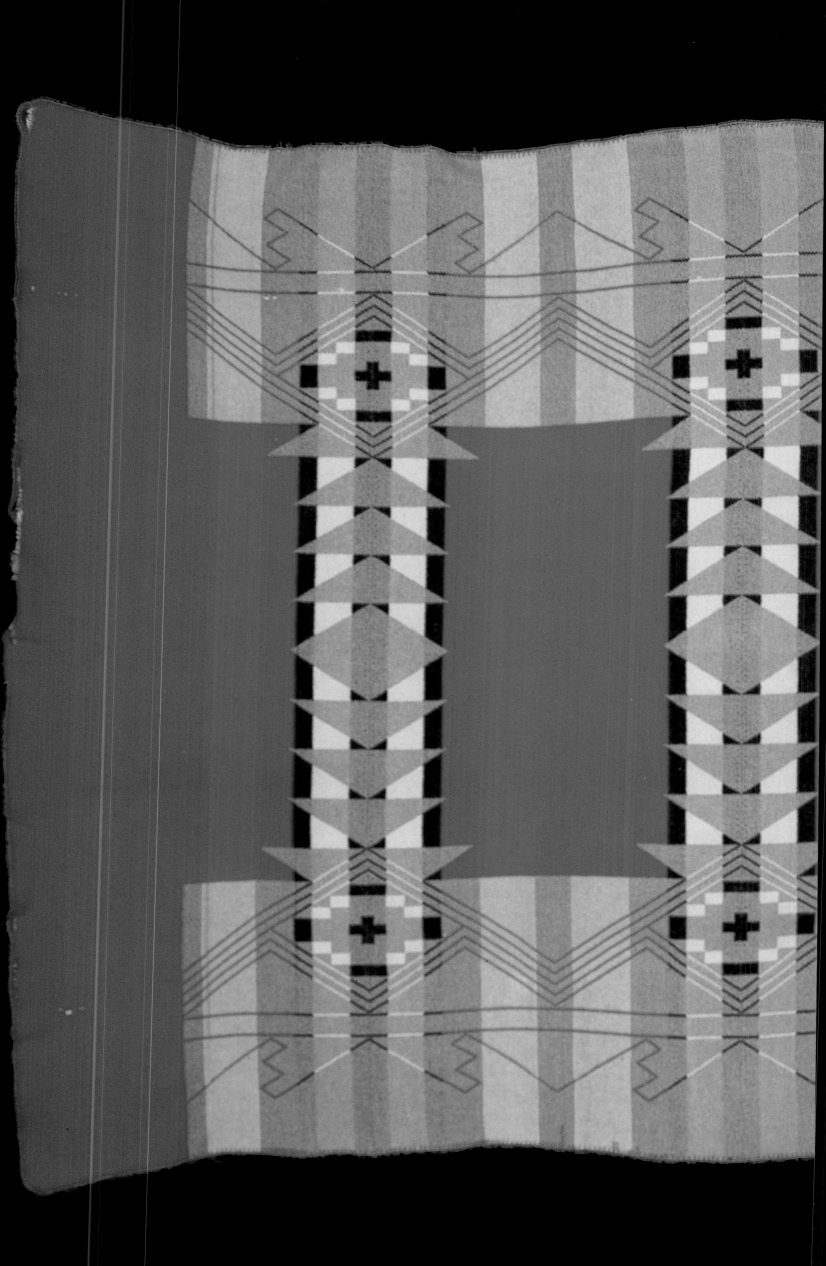

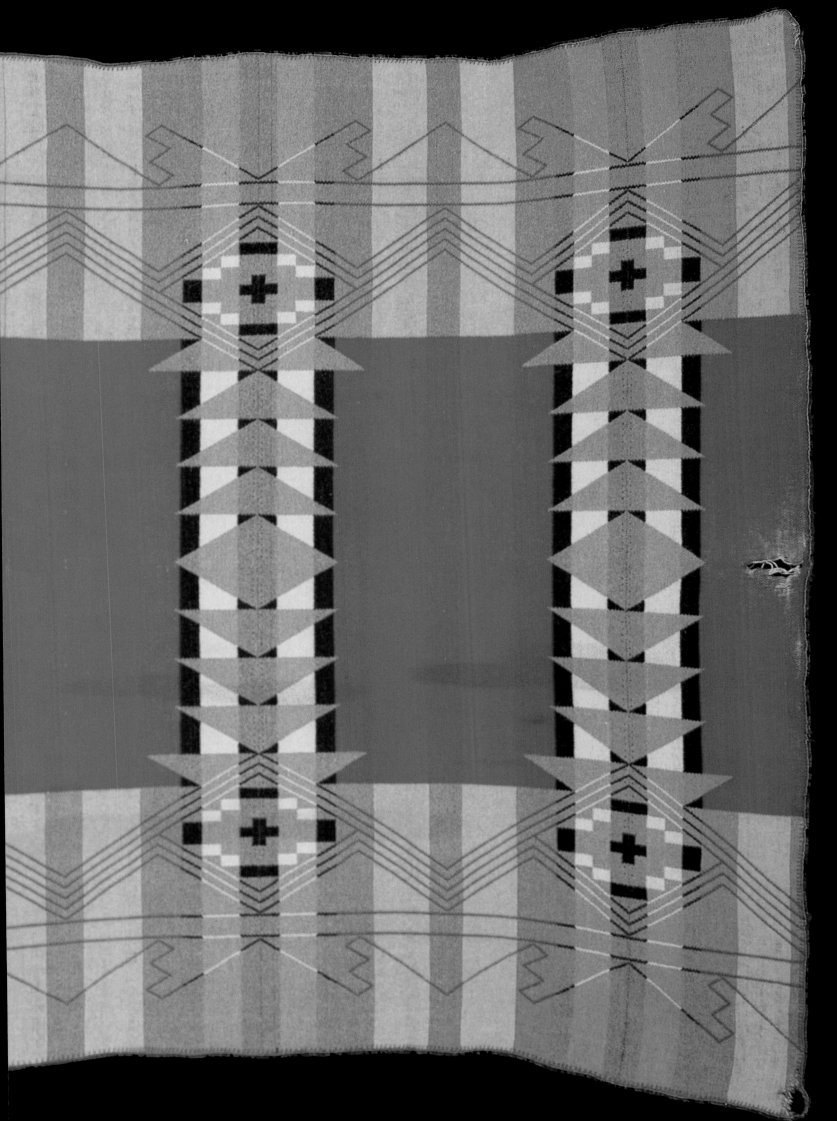

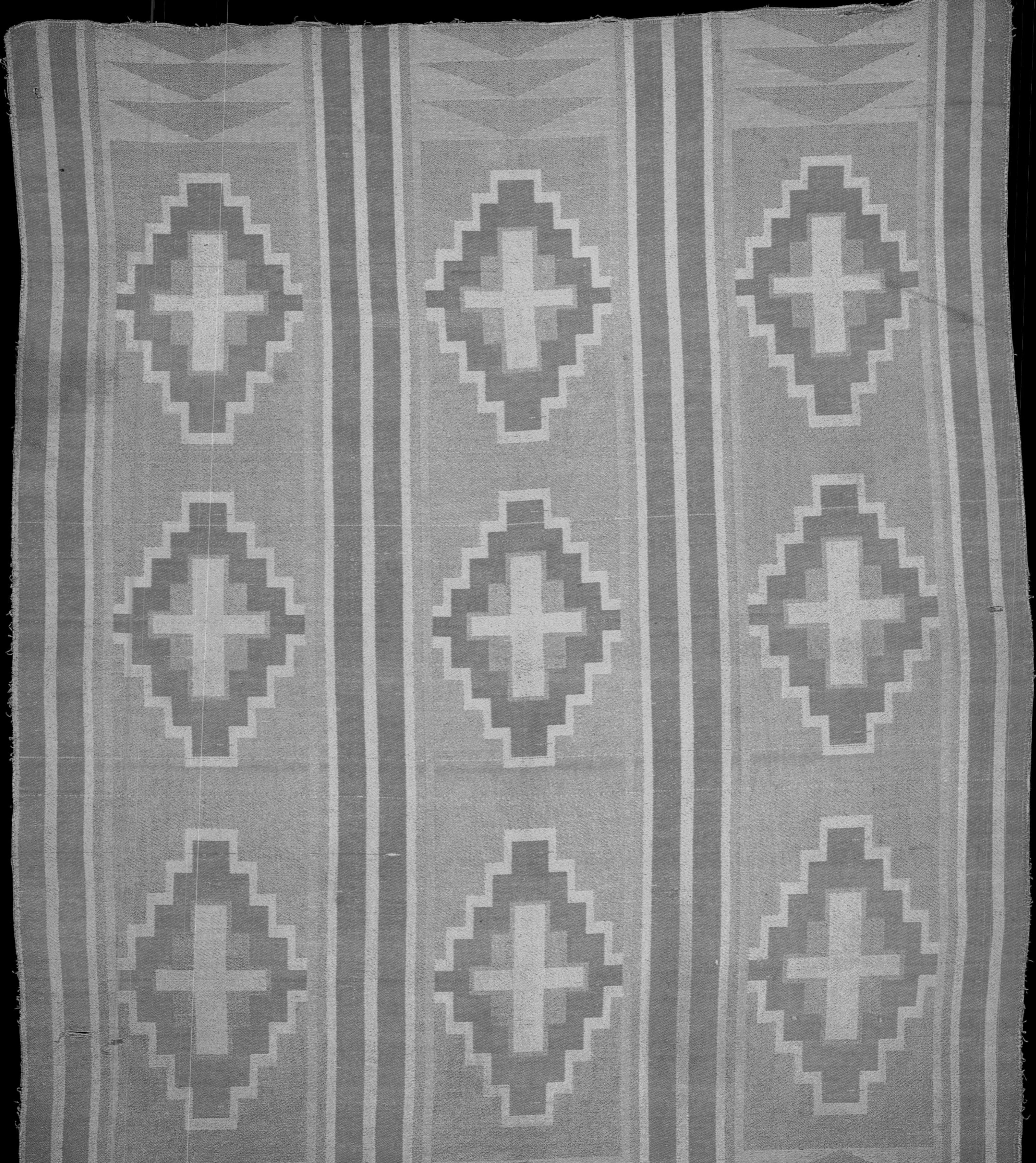

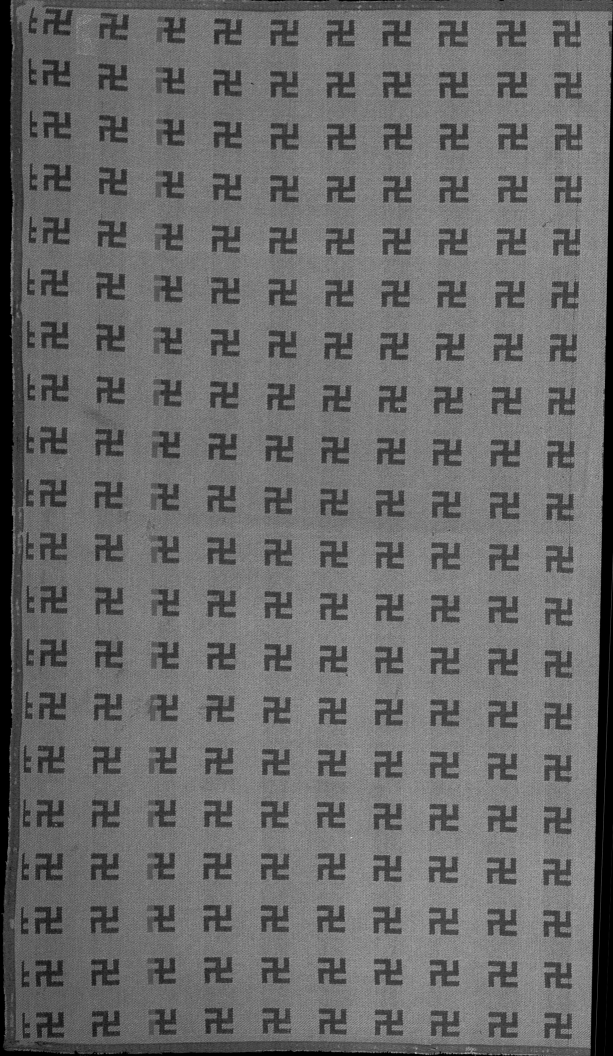

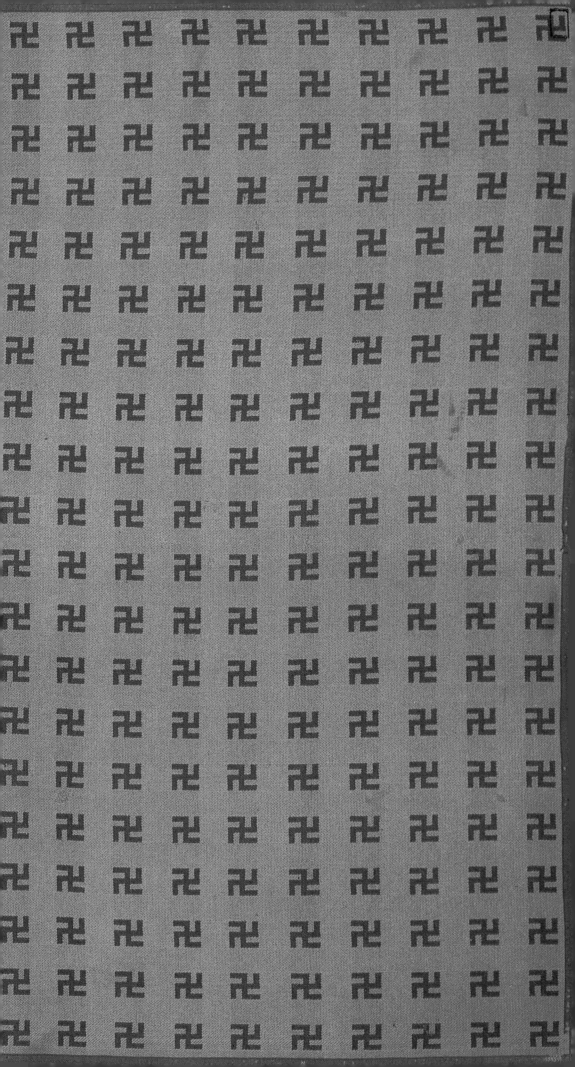

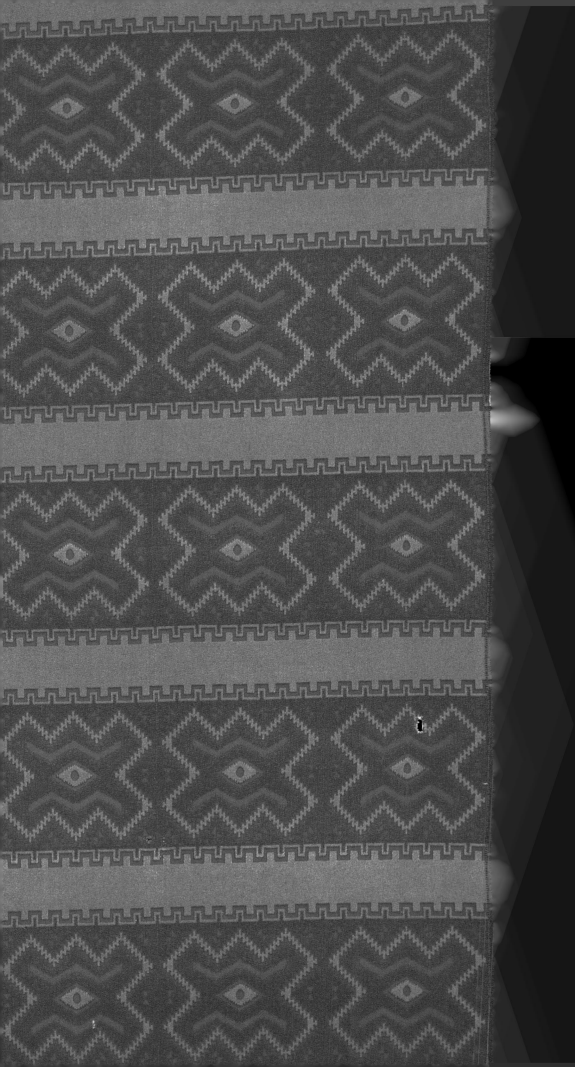

portrayed the American Indian as noble savage. Tapping into the same vein of romanticism, trade blanket manufacturer J. Capps and Sons, of Jacksonville, Illinois, informed all non-Indian customers that to wrap up in a warm and colorful Capps blanket was to realize "a dream of the far prairie and a covered fire." Buffalo Bill himself endorsed Capps products, and the company's 1913 catalog featured a photograph of Buffalo Bill with a group of his Indian employees wearing Capps blankets. His testimonial read:

I am pleased to say, that for characteristic Indian designs, beauty and brilliancy of color, and for quality, the "Capps Indian" blanket is superior to any blanket that I am acquainted with, made for the Indian trade.

COLONEL WM. F. "BUFFALO BILL" CODY, JULY 28, 1911

Buffalo Bill's words testify not only to the quality of the Capps blankets, but also to the marketing acumen of the firm that promoted itself as "Blanket Makers to the Indian Tribes." Homebound readers back East could see actors from the Wild West show modeling blankets covered in striking patterns created by the riotous blends of reds, blues, and oranges. To acquire a Capps blanket and display it in your home was to own a piece of the vanishing romance of the American West and to achieve the blissful harmony of the Noble Red Man—or that's what the advertising promised.

The Capps company produced a number of blanket designs that incorporated the centuries-old, traditional whirling logs design, later called the swastika. Of course, when Capps was designing and producing its blankets, the symbol, also known as "four directions in motion," had yet to take on the horrific association with Nazi Germany in World War II.

Between 1890 and 1917, Capps attributed "an important volume of business" to the manufacture of blankets for sale to federal Indian agents on western reservations, yet the history of the firm (published in its centennial year of 1939) offers less than one of its twenty-nine pages to the discussion of the Indian blanket business.

Buell Manufacturing Company
The Original Power Loom Manufacturers of Indian Robes

Buell, based in St. Louis, Missouri, was the only one of the major trade blanket manufacturers to produce three-color blankets. These blankets—known as the "Cheyenne" and "Shoshoni" designs—were heavier than most trade blankets, because each horizontal line included three colors of yarn rather than the standard two. Buell developed a weaving sleight of hand that enabled it to place the third strand of yarn between the other two to hide that strand from view, or it could create a more complex design using the third color as an option. A robe could thus exhibit three colors in a horizontal band that normally would have shown only two.

Buell marketed three trade blankets with designs based directly on earlier traditional Native American weaving styles. These were "Honolchadi," a third-phase chief's blanket design; "Zuni," a striped Hopi manta design; and "Shoshoni," based on a regional Navajo weaving style.

Racine Woolen Mills
The Indian's Instinct Has Become the White Man's Reasoning Choice

Around 1915, John S. Hart, owner of Racine Woolen Mills (located in Racine, Wisconsin, south of Milwaukee on Lake Michigan), proclaimed to a newspaper reporter that his firm could claim more than forty Indian tribes as regular customers. On a selling trip through the Southwest, John Hart's father, Sands Hart, noticed that Indian people from different tribes chose to wear brightly colored trade blankets "instead of conventional clothing." "The Indian's love for gaudy colors and loose garments despite all the civilization that the white man has forced upon him, retains for the Racine Woolen Mills a very valuable source of income." From a contemporary viewpoint, the company's promotional concepts seem rather racist and strangely condescending, especially considering that popularity among Indian customers was essential for success in the larger non-Indian market.

Fancy shawls were another characteristic product of the Racine Woolen Mills. These shawls were similar to trade blankets in design and construction, but they almost always measured closer to square and always featured fringed edges. Among American Indian people, these fringed shawls were worn exclusively by women. In many photographs from the reservation era, the fringed shawls worn by the women are from the Racine Woolen Mills.

Oregon City Woolen Mills
Perfectly Woven "Navajo Art-Craft" Fabric

Dating its origins back to 1864, Oregon City was one of the older of the major manufacturers of American Indian trade blankets. The company opened its first sales agency in New York in the 1890s, and during its heyday, Oregon City was a major competitor of Pendleton Woolen Mills. In fact, the two firms struggled to dominate the Indian blanket trade. Following World War I, when Racine Woolen Mills, Buell Manufacturing Company, and J. Capps and Sons were no longer manufacturing trade blankets, Oregon City still played a major role. The mill was located near the falls of the Willamette River, south of Portland, Oregon.

A 1914 Oregon City catalog proclaimed that "we have naturally reproduced the Indian's most cherished patterns. Our designers are men steeped in Indian lore. They have worked side-by-side with the Indian and come into possession of his favorite designs and colorings, along with their symbolism."

The company told a romantic story of itself and its product:

Closely interwoven with the history of Oregon is the history of the Indian—his onslaughts, his brave battles, his retreat, and in the end the pitiful vanquishment of a noble race. To the Indian, everything is symbolic. The brilliant, resplendent colors so dear to his heart are an expression of his interpretations of Life—the green of the earth, the blue of the heavens, the flight of a flock of birds, the sweep of the winds and the splash of the waves. We are preserving the rare charm of Indian weaving by modern methods. All the beauty and significance originally woven into fabric by the Indian, on his crude hand loom, are retained in our perfectly woven Navajo Art-Craft fabrics.

Actually, there was little that could really be called "traditional" about the designs for Oregon City blankets, but the company produced beautifully designed and well-woven trade blankets.

Oregon City created a successful business strategy. Its retail stores in the West and Midwest prospered through the 1920s, and the company even made significant inroads into the lucrative southwestern market and C. N. Cotton's trading company. But during the Depression, the chain of stores shrank to just four—in Seattle, Portland, San Francisco, and Tacoma.

Pendleton Woolen Mills

The Wild Indian's Overcoat

Pendleton is undoubtedly the most recognized name in American Indian trade blankets. The original mill was located in Oregon, and its name became synonymous with quality across the United States. When C. N. Cotton established his regional wholesale business in Gallup, New Mexico, he illustrated his business acumen by "obtaining exclusive regional control of two items basic to the Navajo Trade: Arbuckle's Coffee and Pendleton Blankets. To most Navajos of that time, any coffee or blanket under another name was either counterfeit or an inferior substitute."[6] This unqualified endorsement helped to ensure Pendleton's success, and it is the only surviving company among the five major manufacturers of American Indian trade blankets that flourished in the early 1900s.

Pendleton produced its first catalog around 1901, a three-by-five-inch brochure featuring a cover photograph of a be-robed Nez Percé Chief Joseph, and titled "The Story of the Wild Indian's Overcoat." The company emphasized its associations with the American Indian people in its marketing programs and made an effort to describe native traditions and customs in its advertising literature. As was typical of the period, the information was at best romanticized and at worst racist:

This reservation [the Umatilla] is recognized not only as a social center, but as the emporium of Indian fashion. What a Paris hat is to a Chicago girl on Easter morning, a Pendleton robe is to the debutante of every reservation from Arizona to the Dakotas. The Umatilla buck is a fashion plate. . . .

She [Mrs. Yellow Hawk] is a lady of judgement, she is willing to pay a good price for a Pendleton robe, knowing that it will be bright and serviceable long after the cheaper grades have been thrown aside for saddle blankets. . . .

Our pale-face trade is not unlike that with the red man. We make robes in college colors, crimson and white, orange and black, crimson with navy blue, etc., each college town preparing its own colors. . . .

The Pendleton Woolen Mills virtually transformed itself with the purchase of its first Jacquard loom in July 1901. The company's management couldn't have known how important the decision would be for the future of the company, but the timing could not have been more fortunate. Because the Jacquard loom, a French invention, was so advanced, a specially trained technician accompanied it to the installation site. For the Pendleton project, serendipity brought Englishman Joseph Rawnsley to Oregon along with the impressive machine. Much to Pendleton's good fortune, he didn't go home. Rawnsley took over the development of Indian designs for the company and continued his association until his death in 1929. During the course of his career, he traveled widely among the American Indian people. Rawnsley created many of the most popular blanket designs, and he was the only blanket designer to gain individual notice. One measure of his success is the high percentage of blankets that Pendleton still sells to Native Americans. In fact, Pendleton notes that currently it sells at least half of its production of blankets to the American Indian population.

The technology of the Jacquard double-shuttle loom used so effectively by Rawnsley enabled all the mills to produce the more colorful and intricate designs typical of the uniquely American trade blankets. The older looms—such as those on which the early Hudson's Bay blankets were woven in England—could weave a blanket with only one color of yarn, so they were unable to alternate colors in a single horizontal row. As a result, the early trade blankets were simple striped designs like that of the Hudson's Bay blanket.

The Jacquard loom could alternate yarn colors on each individual row of the blanket, so that the blanket could present a doubled-sided image. The designs were essentially the same on both sides of the blanket, but the colors alternated. One way to distinguish the two blanket sides is to refer to the side where the pattern is dominant as the "patternization" side. The side opposite the "patternization" side will show the color dominant, and is called the "colorization" side. The Buell Manufacturing Company, as already noted, developed a technique to weave with three yarn colors on a single row. The third color was essentially hidden between the other two colors so the design could be the same on both sides. This was particularly important for the Buell designs that more closely represented traditional Navajo weaving designs.

A sense of competition and the urge to provide the most innovative designs to the Indian and non-Indian markets kept the blanket companies creative and tested the limits of their technical ability. World War I was a turning point for the industry, as companies turned their production capacity to meeting wartime demands. Oregon City maintained its production of trade blankets until it ceased operation in the late 1920s. Following the closure of the Oregon City operation, Pendleton emerged as the market leader.

Now, at the turn of a new century, trade blankets are still valued as gifts on special occasions and are much in evidence at social and ceremonial gatherings. Special, limited editions and commemorative designs are popular as well. A few small companies, including one that specializes in producing blankets from Navajo-grown wool, have made an impact on the market, but Pendleton Woolen Mills remains the leader. The name Pendleton is still synonymous with American Indian trade blankets.

Poetry in Motion

The future will present another chapter based on the interwoven plotlines of design, commerce, and Native American people constituting the history of the American Indian trade blanket. New weaving technology allows even greater flexibility in design. Native American artists have taken a greater interest in textile design and are collaborating with Pendleton to produce unique designs for trade blankets.

Contemporary blanket designs are being inspired by all kinds of influences, from baskets and basket designs to classic Navajo weavings. They convey the power of ideas, and they represent the life that people transfer to the objects they revere.

The fact that trade blankets are machine-made and not handwoven has never prevented them from occupying an important place in the history of weaving. They have been integral to the lives of many groups of North America's indigenous people. It is important to remember that trade blankets are functional items made beautiful not only by those who design and produce them, but also by those who wear, use, and appreciate them.

These blankets have transcended the strictly utilitarian roles that might have been assigned to them originally. They eagerly offer flashes of color and texture to all those open to experiencing them. While trade blanket designs may demand a unique humanist, creative sensibility that enables the viewer to find beauty in unexpected places, they amply reward the effort.

139

[1] John C. Ewers, *The Blackfeet: Raiders on the Northwestern Plains* (Norman: University of Oklahoma Press, 1958), 69.

[2] Patrick W. Houlihan, foreword to *The Language of the Robe*, by Robert W. Kapoun with Charles J. Lohrmann (Layton, Utah: Peregrine Smith, 1992), vii.

[3] Ibid.

[4] Rain Parrish, "A Woman's Experience," in *The Language of the Robe*, 2.

[5] Hubert Howe Bancroft, *History of the Northwest Coast*, vol. 1, *1543–1800* (San Francisco: A. L. Bancroft and Co., 1884), 466–67.

[6] Frank McNitt, *The Indian Traders* (Norman: University of Oklahoma Press, 1962), 222.

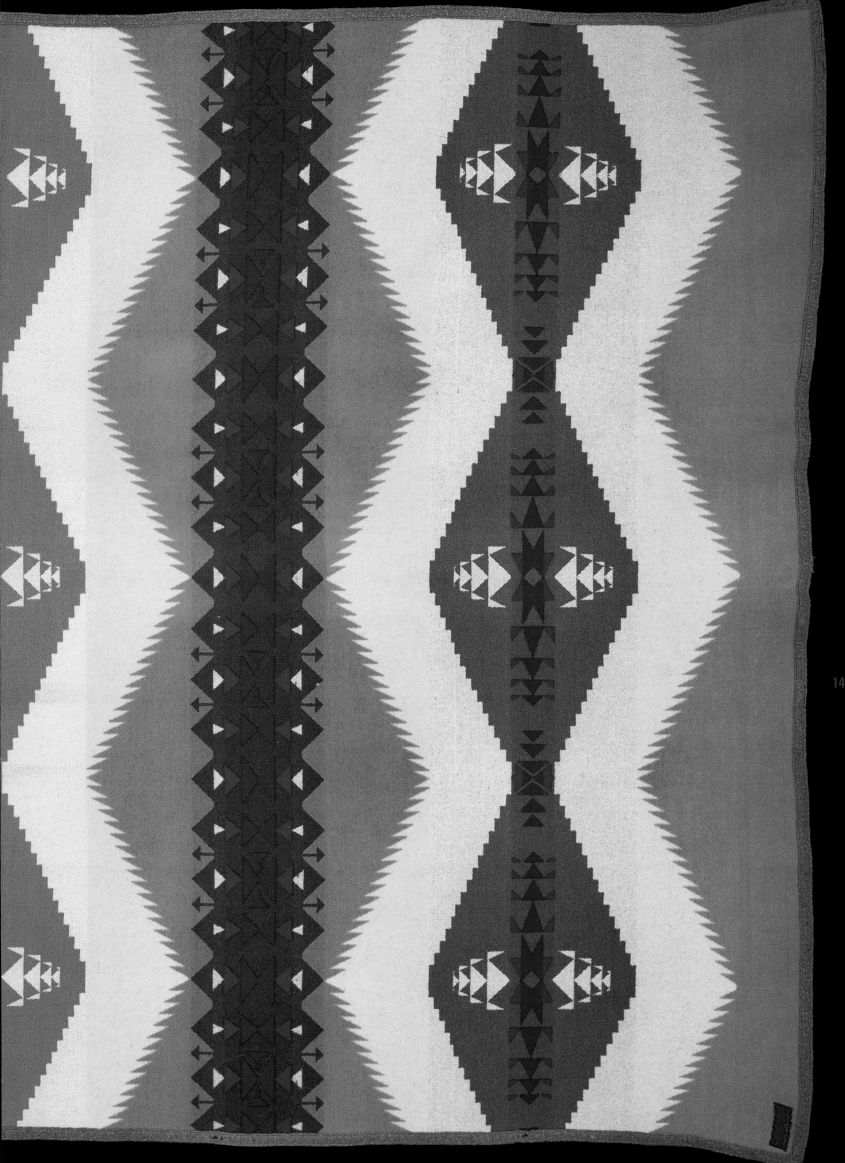

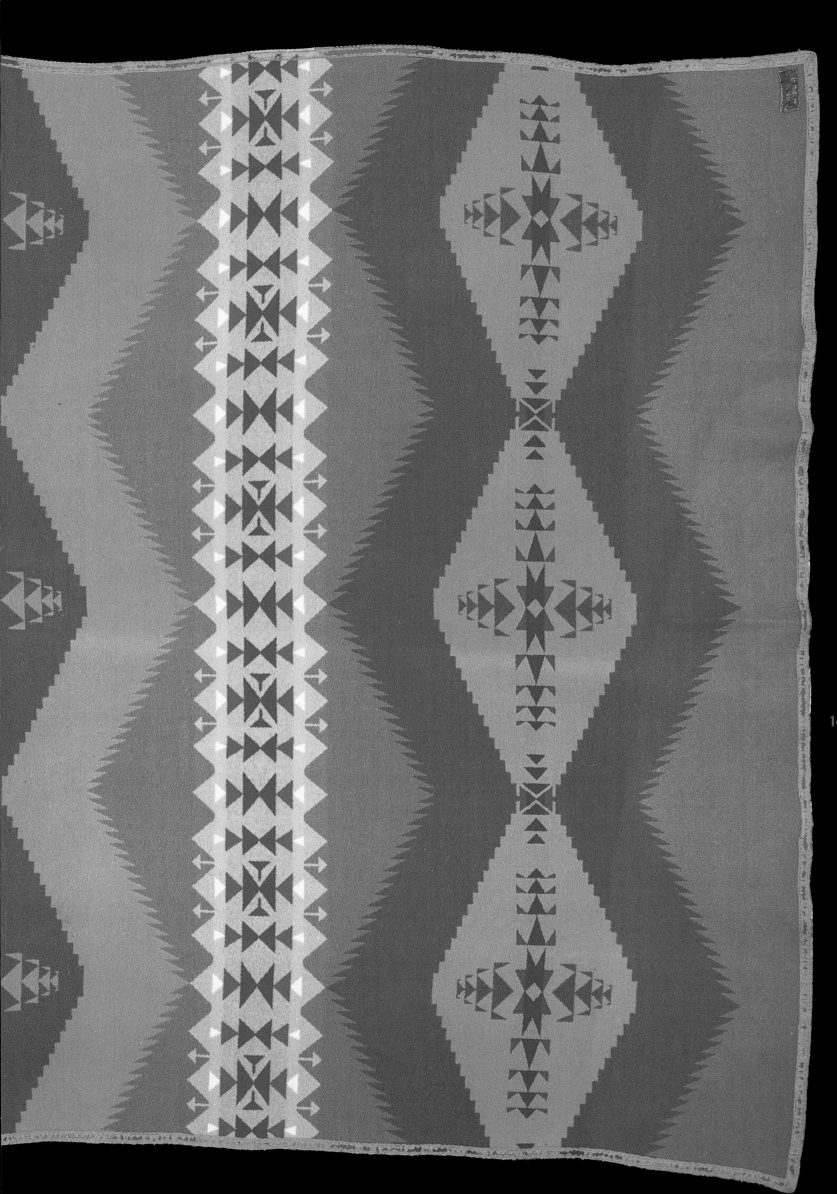

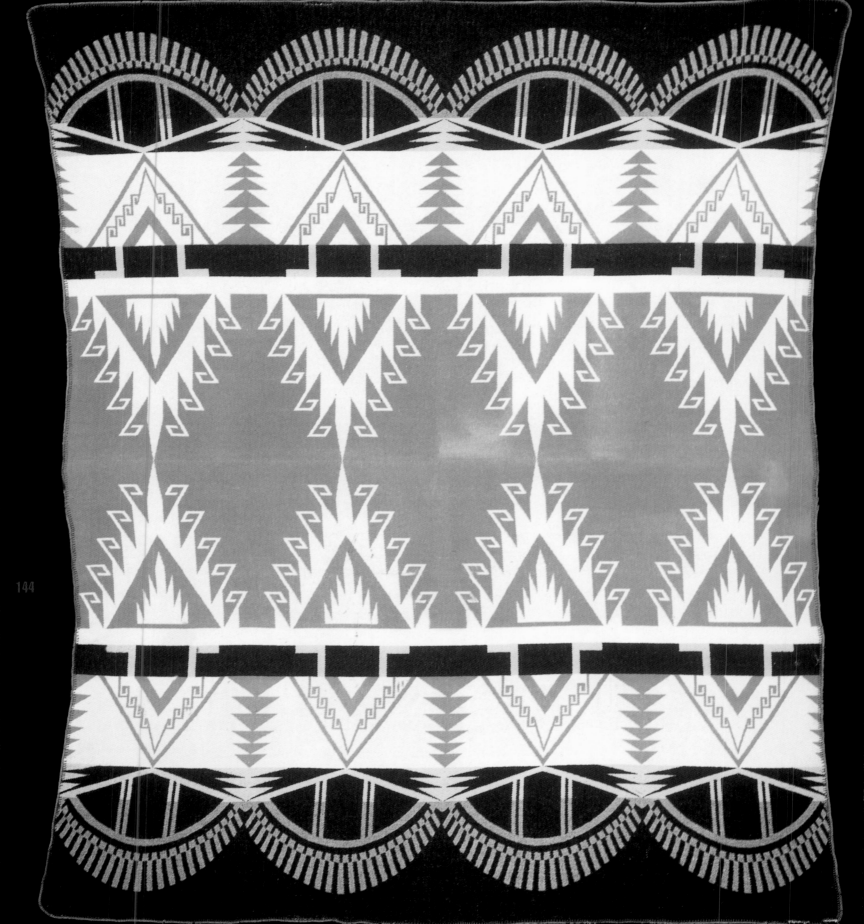

144

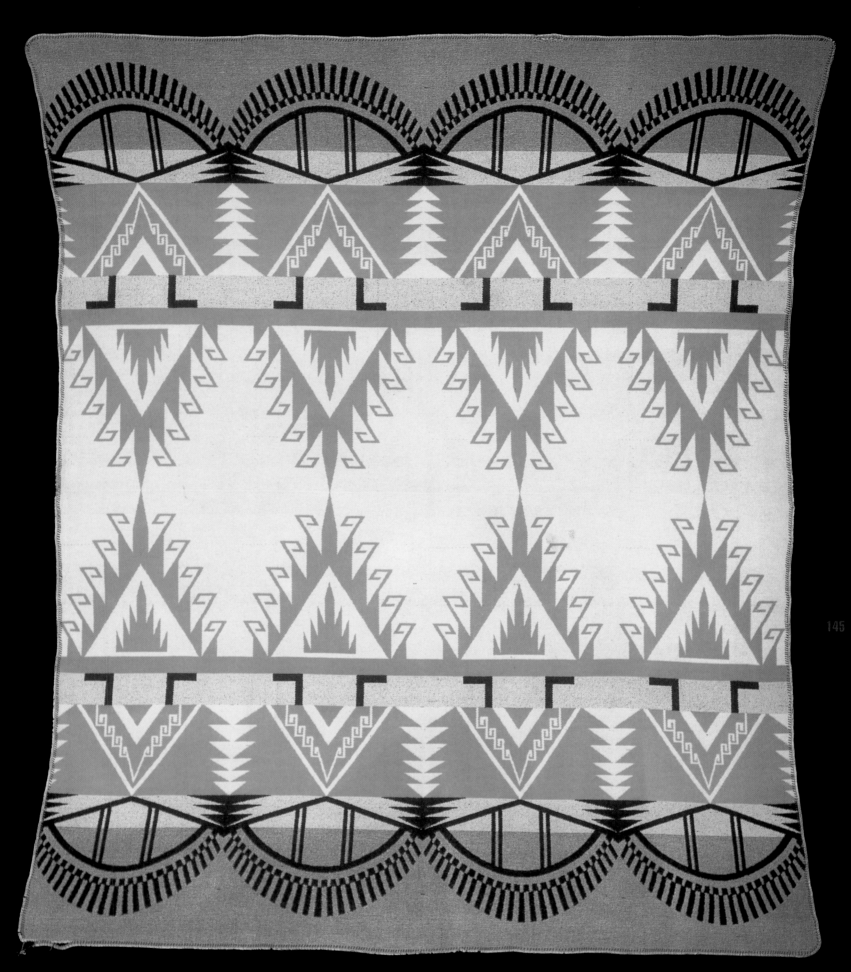

146

MAJOR MOORHOUSE

Pendl

und Up
n Oregon

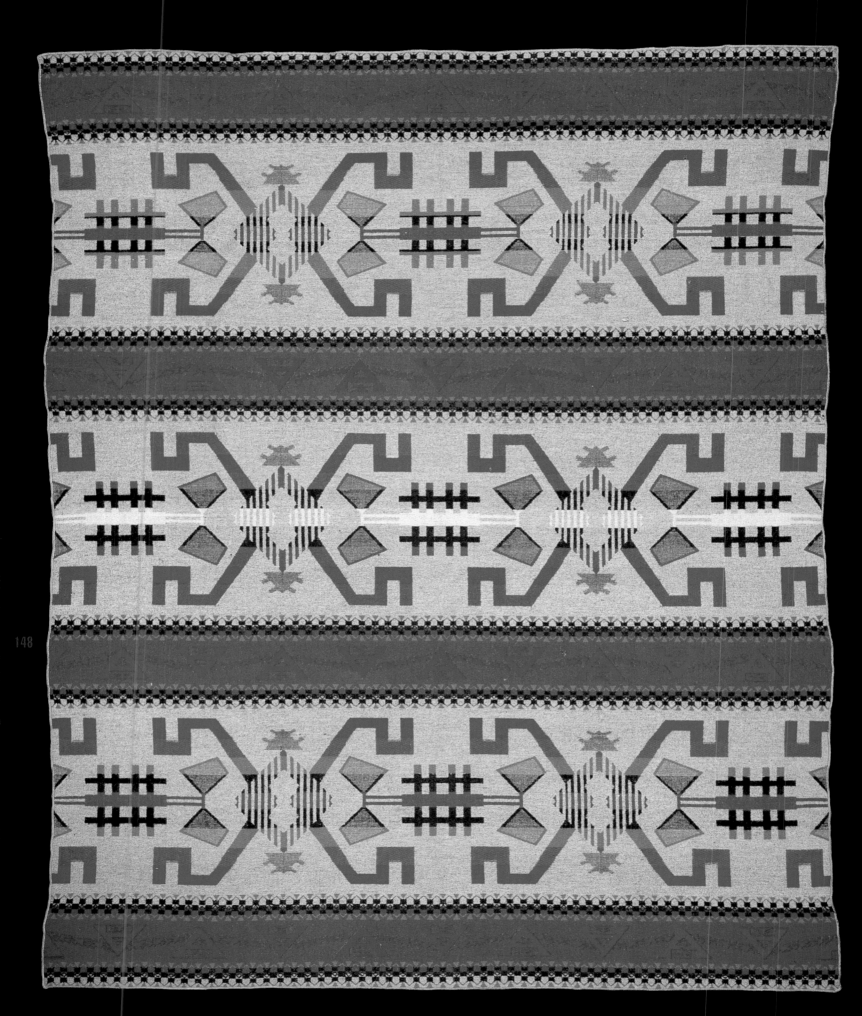

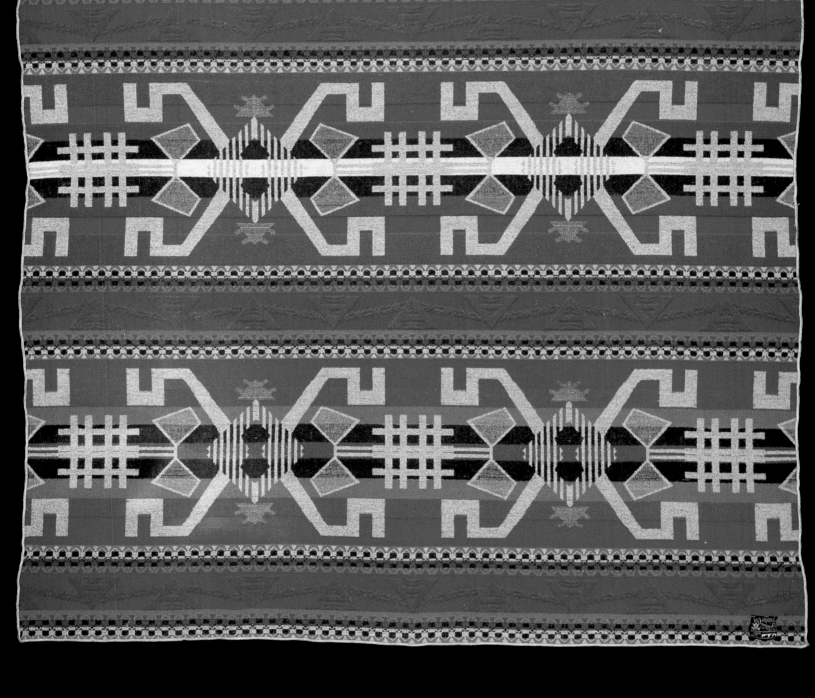

149

153

155

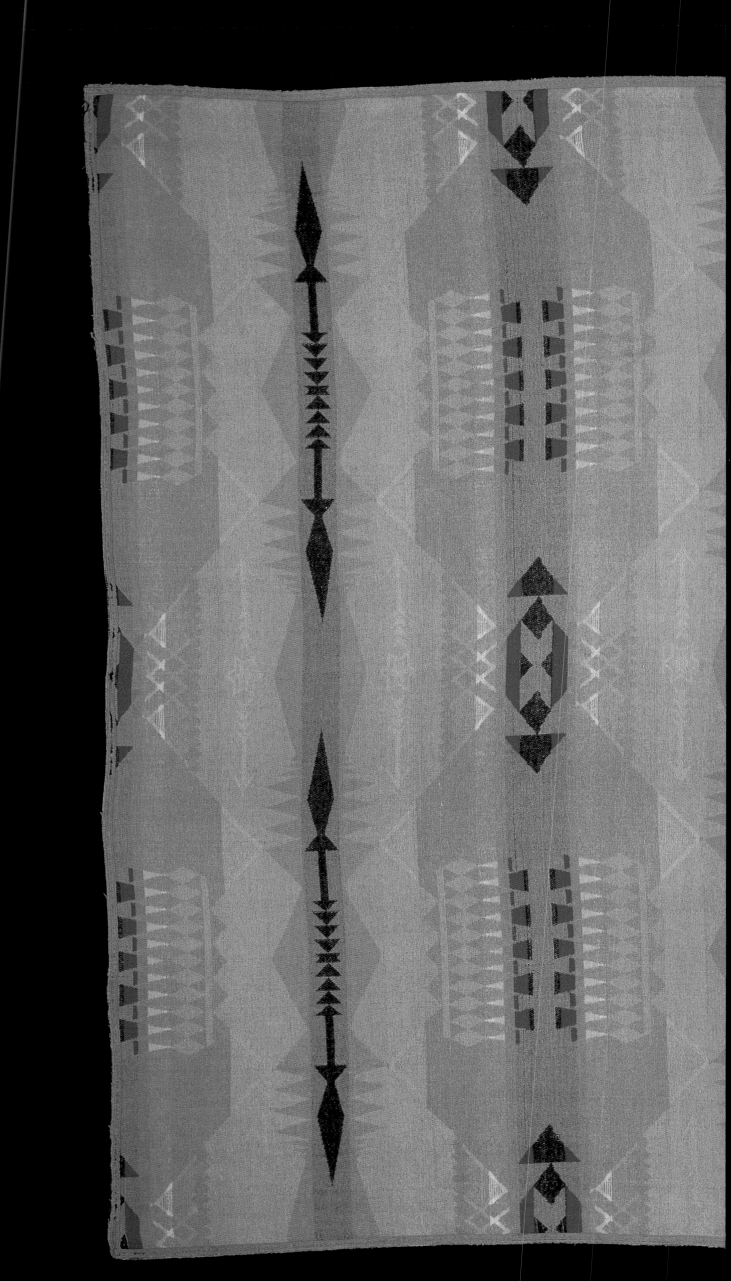

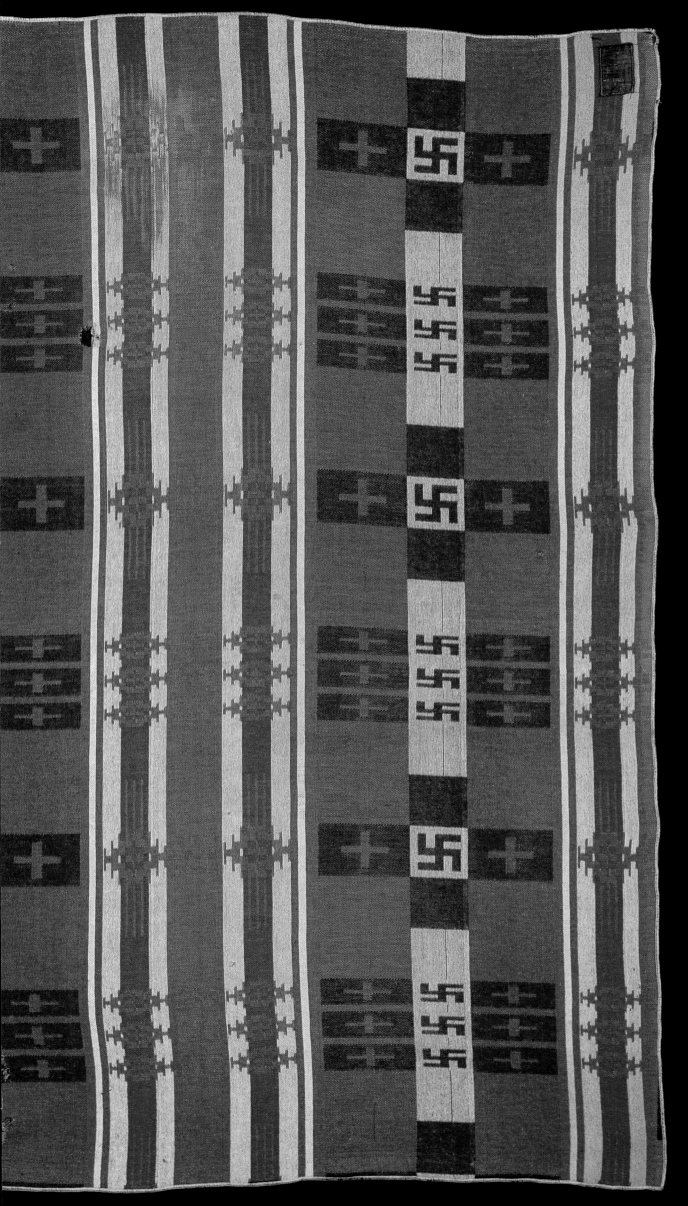

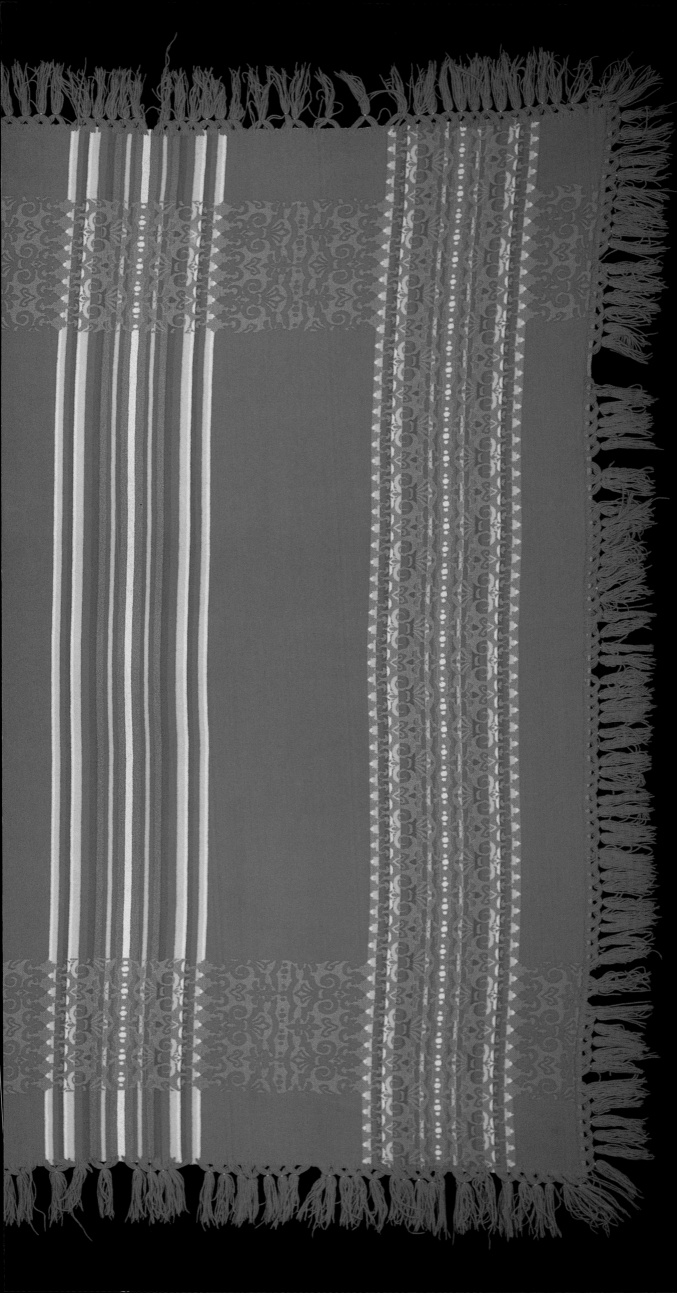

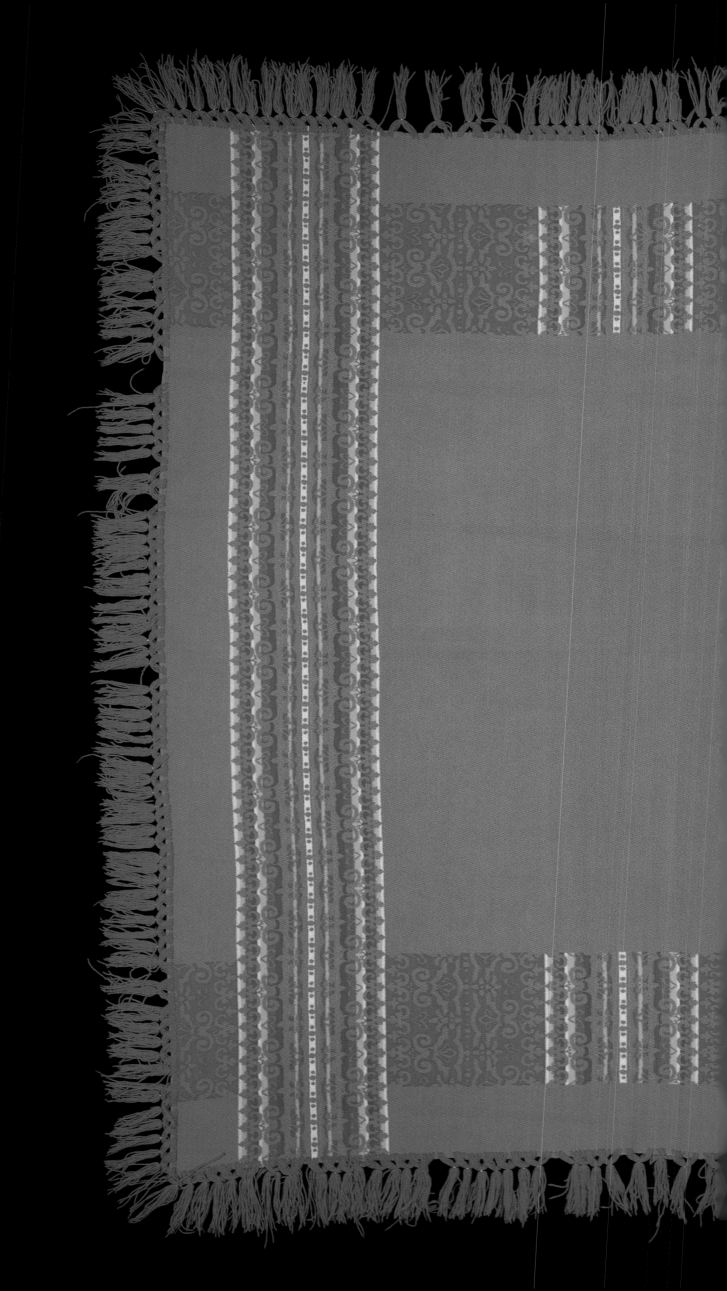

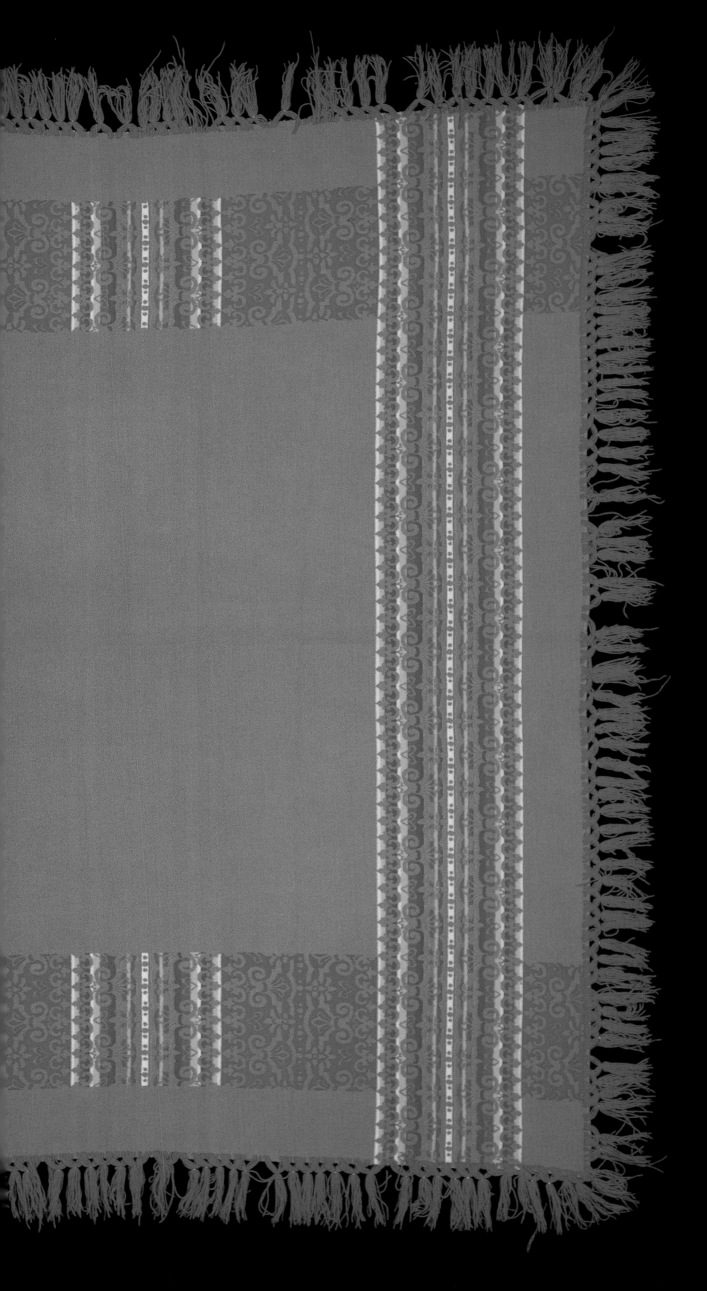

163

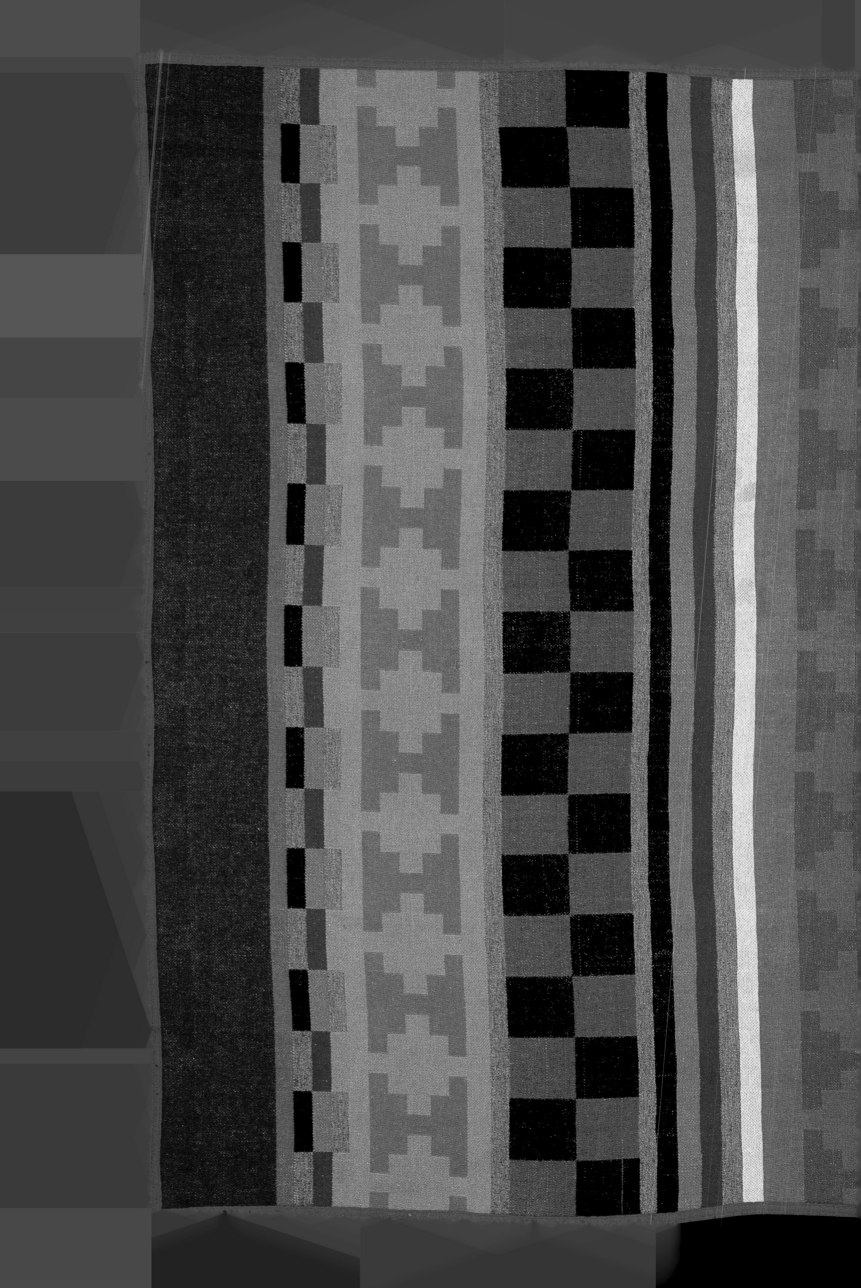

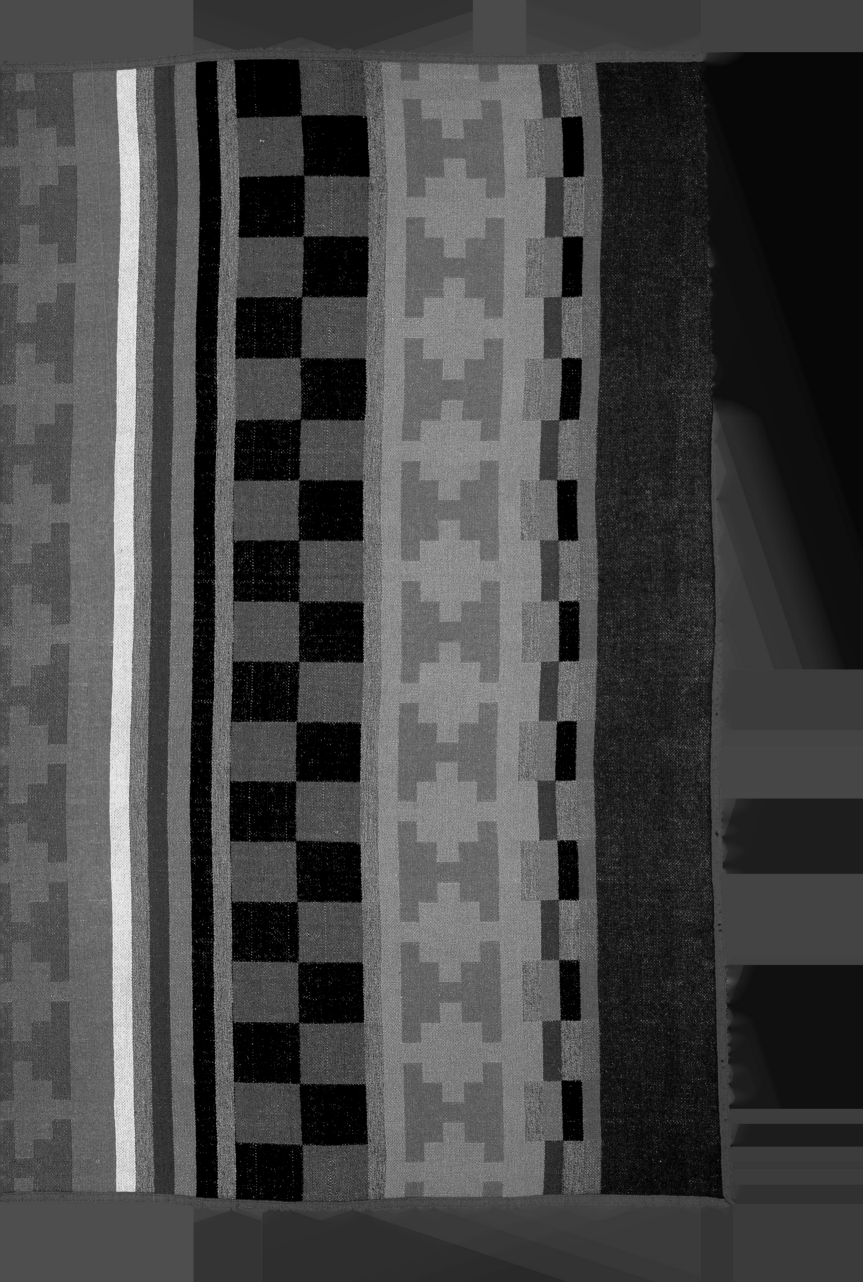

171

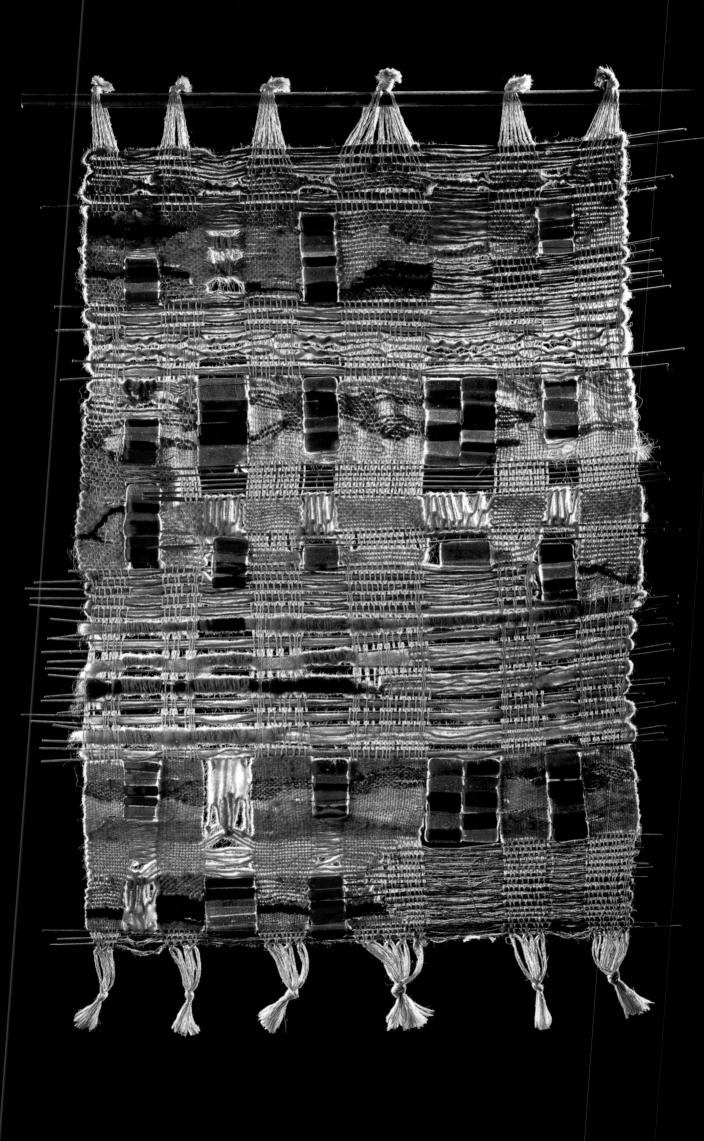

The Indian Influences
Upon My Work

My first serious use of glass consisted of my weaving small pieces of glass into tapestries. This was during my junior and senior years at the University of Washington (1963–65). After studying weaving and textiles, I wound up falling in love with both Navajo blankets and Pendleton trade blankets. As a student, I couldn't afford the Navajo blankets, but I began to collect Pendletons. This was the beginning of my involvement with Native American design. I probably got as much pleasure from my Pendleton collection as I would have from Navajo blankets. ■ A turning point came in 1974. That year, I built a glass shop for the Institute of American Indian Art in Santa Fe, visited the first major exhibition of Navajo blankets (at the Museum of Fine Arts in Boston), and, along with Jamie Carpenter and Italo Scanga, developed a drawing pickup technique that led to the creation of my *Navajo Blanket Cylinders* (in late 1974). We created drawings inspired by Indian blanket designs, using glass threads that we then picked up onto the surface of the hot cylinders. The pickup technique lent itself very nicely to making geometric patterns, as many simple techniques do. Traditional Navajo weavers, for example, used very basic weaving techniques to produce their geometric designs. Pendleton blankets, on the other hand, were made on far more sophisticated looms. These looms could, and occasionally did, produce very complex and organic designs. The complex designs were rarely used, however, because the Pendletons were supposed to imitate or suggest the traditional Navajo blankets. Thus, most Pendletons were simple, geometric, and very beautiful. Pendleton did take more liberty with color, given the vast availability of colored yarns. These yarns were generally not available to the Indians, who would have surely used the bright colors had they had access to them. The unusual colors were one of the major attractions for the Indians—they often preferred wearing the Pendletons to their own handwoven blankets. ■ I blew the *Navajo Blanket Cylinders* for two years, and then started making the *Baskets*. The *Baskets* were influenced by Northwest Coast Indian baskets that I had seen at the Washington State Historical Museum during the summer of 1977. I exhibited the new series for the first time that same year at the Seattle Art Museum—I placed one hundred *Baskets* of all sizes and shapes on a twenty-four-foot-long, diamond-plated steel table. As usual, the *Baskets* were not well accepted by the critics or collectors in the beginning—it took a year or two before collectors started to buy them. Both the drawing pickup technique that had led to the *Navajo Blanket*

Cylinders and a new way of blowing very thin and misshapen basket forms derived from Indian sources. These became two of the most influential series that I created. ■ The *Baskets* went on to inform many of the series that followed. The *Seaforms, Macchia,* and *Soft Cylinders* all came directly from the style of blowing that I had developed for the *Baskets.* This blowing technique was the result of my trying to make the forms appear as natural as possible, using as few tools as I could. I wanted to concentrate on using the fire from the furnace as well as centrifugal force and gravity. This meant letting glass find its own form, so that the pieces could appear very fragile and natural. In exploring ways to make the pieces thinner and stronger, I tried blowing them into ribbed molds that could give them additional strength, like corrugated cardboard. That is how I developed the *Seaforms.* The ribbing and the way it influences the form make the pieces seem shell-like. ■ Much of the surface threading on the *Baskets* and *Seaforms* came directly from what I had learned from making the *Navajo Blanket Cylinders.* In the beginning, the *Navajo Blanket Cylinder* drawings were usually made from thin glass threads that were cut up and put together by Kate Elliott, who had been with us in 1974 when we developed the drawing pickup technique. Kate then learned how to bend the threads with a small torch to make curves, and the blanket designs became more complicated. I became very interested barbed wire, because it had been invented around the same time as the most beautiful Navajo blankets were being woven. I liked using the image of barbed wire within the *Navajo Blanket Cylinders*. Kate was actually able to bend glass threads to make glass barbed wire by knotting it in the same way in which real barbed wire was constructed. ■ In the summer of 1975, I built a glass shop for a new summer art school in Utah called Snowbird. Flora Mace, a recent graduate student in glass from the University of Illinois, enrolled in my program. She was extraordinarily talented with a torch and took the drawing pickup technique to new heights. I could give Flora a photo of a blanket and she could interpret it and make a stunning glass blanket, sometimes spending several hours on the construction. These blowing sessions were some of the most exciting and challenging of my career. The *Navajo Blanket Cylinders* were the largest and most complicated pieces I had ever blown, and Flora's drawings were superb in every way. ■ My painter friend Seaver Leslie came out to Snowbird that summer and helped me blow. He learned the potential of the pickup technique to make drawings, and later that year we produced forty-four *Irish* and *Ulysses Cylinders*. Seaver made graphite drawings illustrating Joyce's novel, and Flora copied them in glass. I blew the cylinders, as did several Rhode Island School of Design students who completed the team. Because of the car accident Seaver and I had in

England a few months later, the *Irish Cylinders* were not shown. Ultimately, the entire series of forty-four was purchased by George Stroemple. They were later exhibited at the Portland Art Museum and are illustrated in the catalogue *Chihuly: The George Stroemple Collection.* ■ Because of the accident, I didn't blow glass for six months. When I started again in late 1976, I began where I had left off with cylinders. But the *Cylinder* series had more or less come to an end. Then (and now), I usually stop a series when I feel I have explored it fully. It wasn't until the summer of 1977, when I happened upon the Northwest Coast Indian baskets, that I began a new body of work, the *Baskets.* ■ In the beginning, the *Baskets* had very little surface decoration, because my main concern was form. Eventually, I started making shard drawings with Flora Mace. The shard drawings were an extension of the earlier technique. Flora made shards by blowing bubbles of intense color, then breaking and cuffing the shards into geometric or semi-geometric shapes. Using her torch, she drew molten threads directly onto the shards. It's a wonderful technique, but it requires very careful preparation in order to pick up each shard without breaking it. Looking back, I think it is possible to say that in both series, the *Navajo Blanket Cylinders* and the *Baskets,* the pieces were wearing their drawings just as the Indians were wearing their blankets.

CYLINDERS 1975-95

183

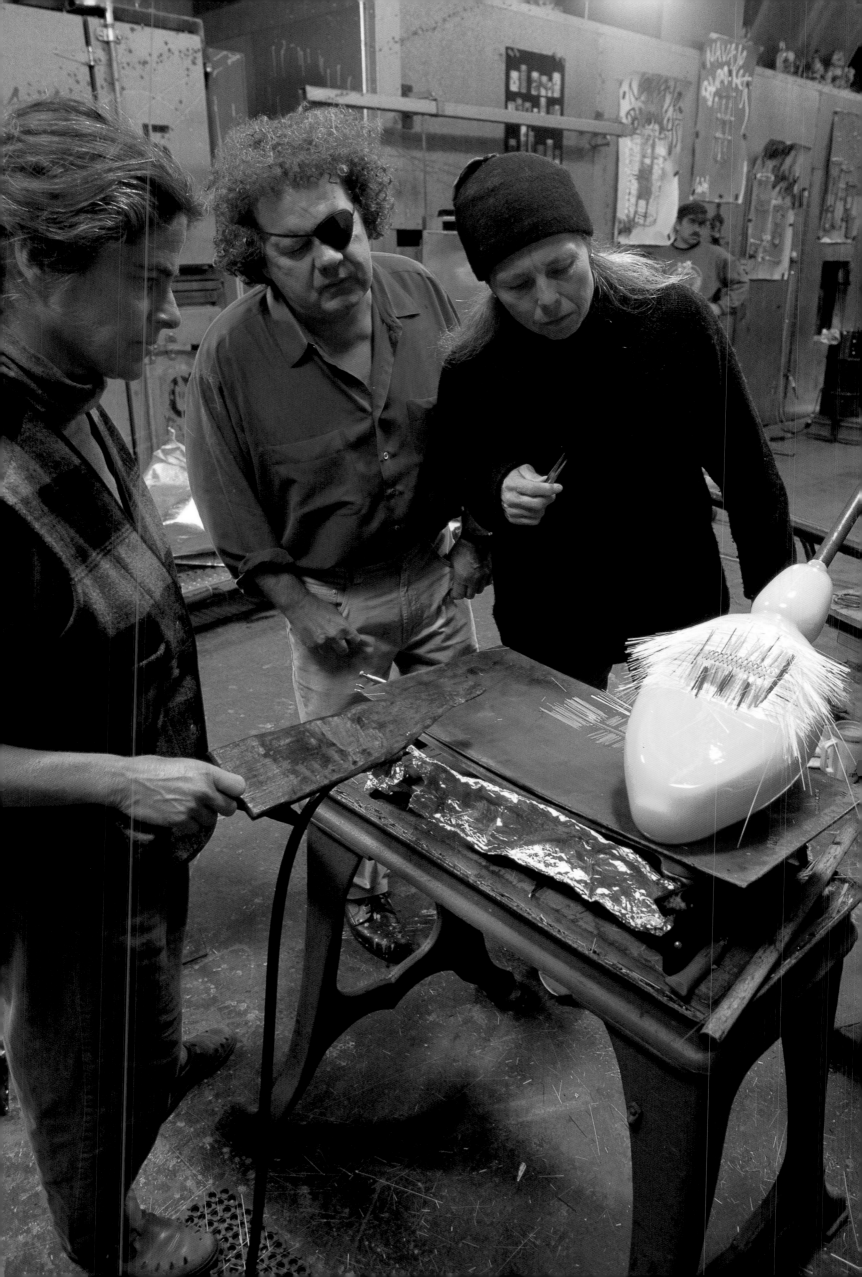

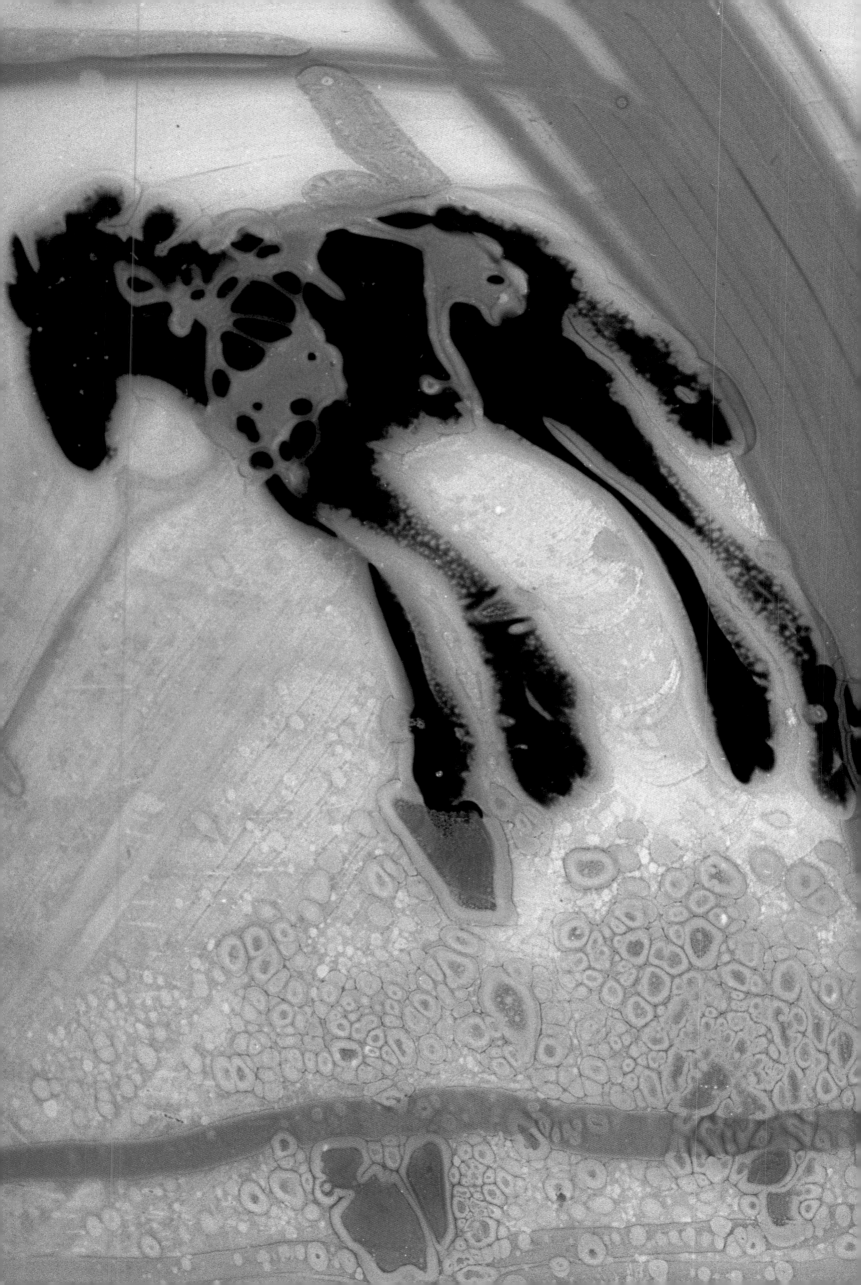

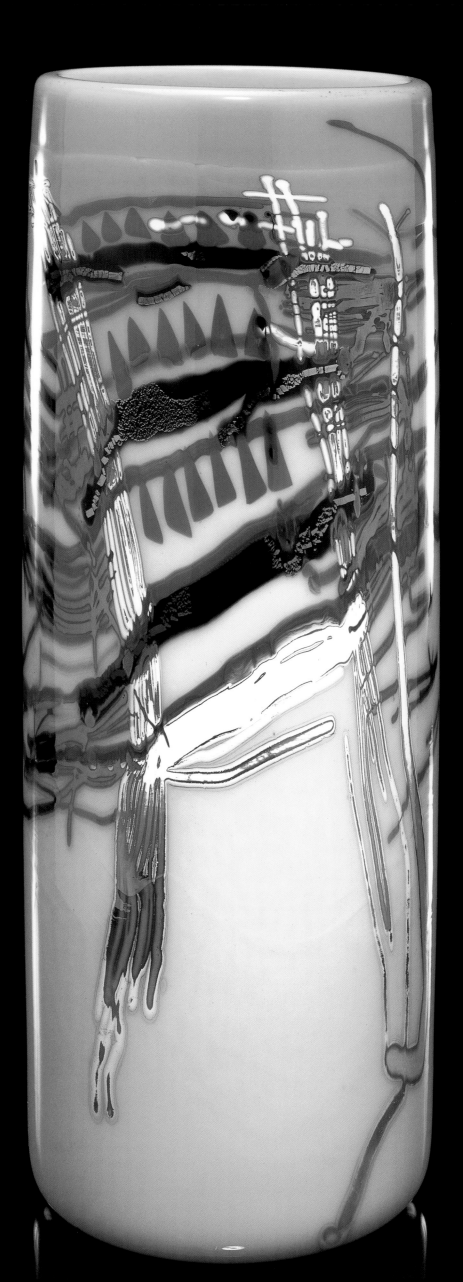

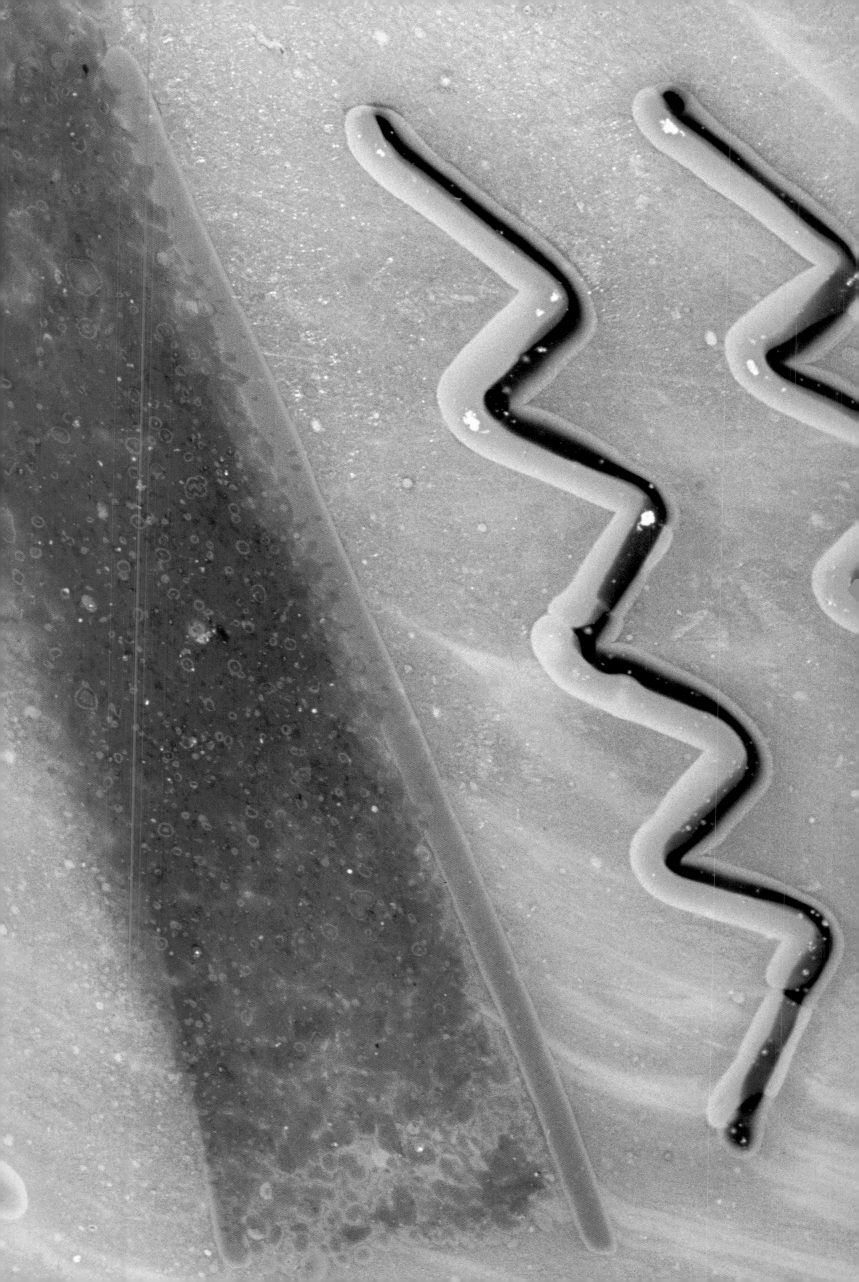

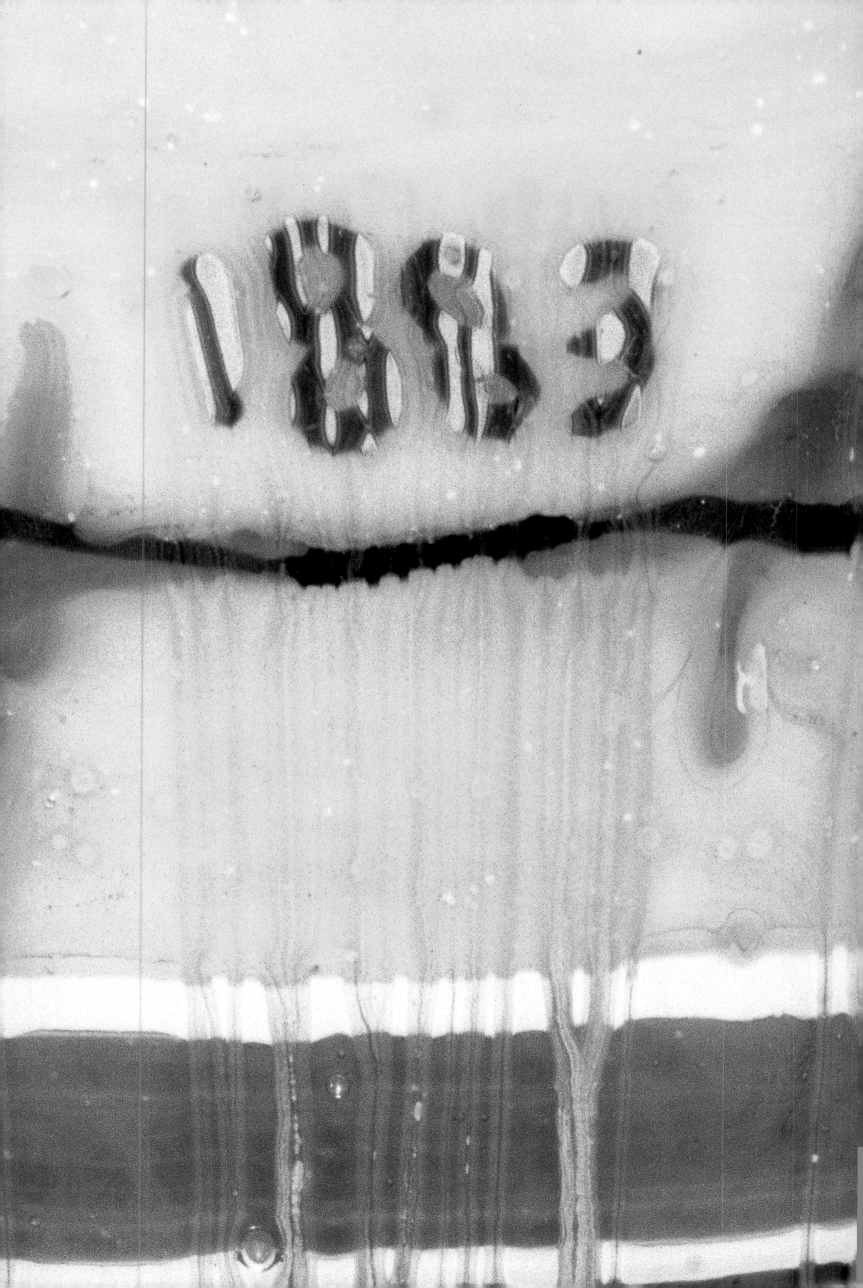

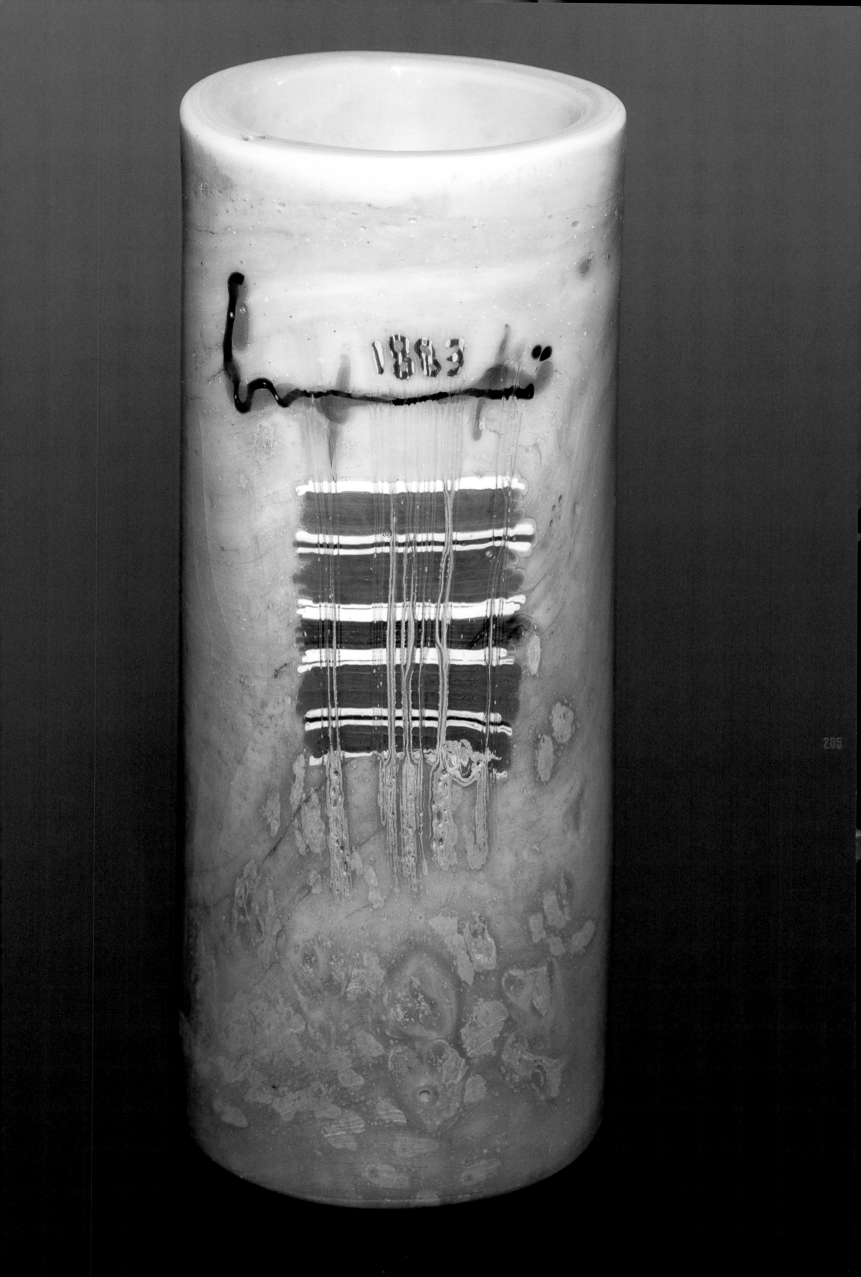

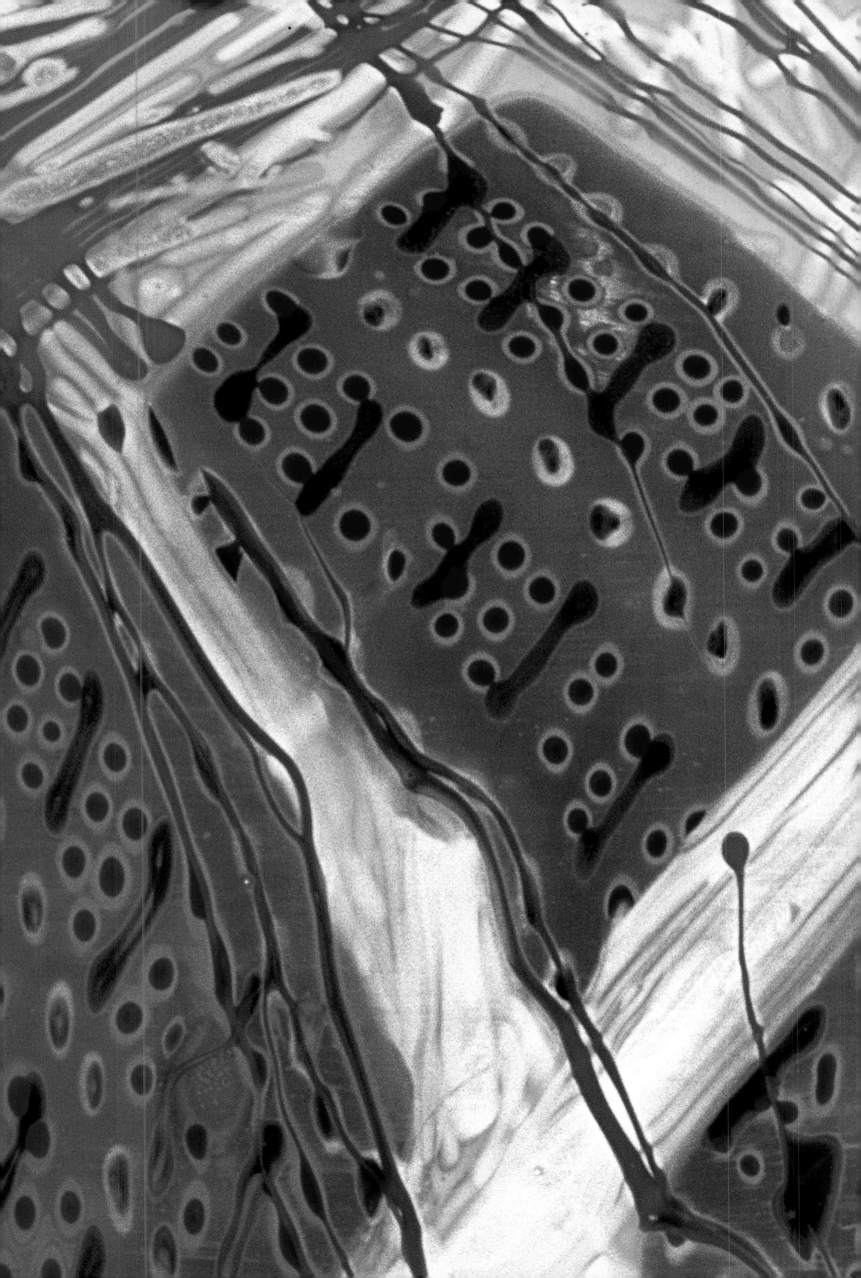

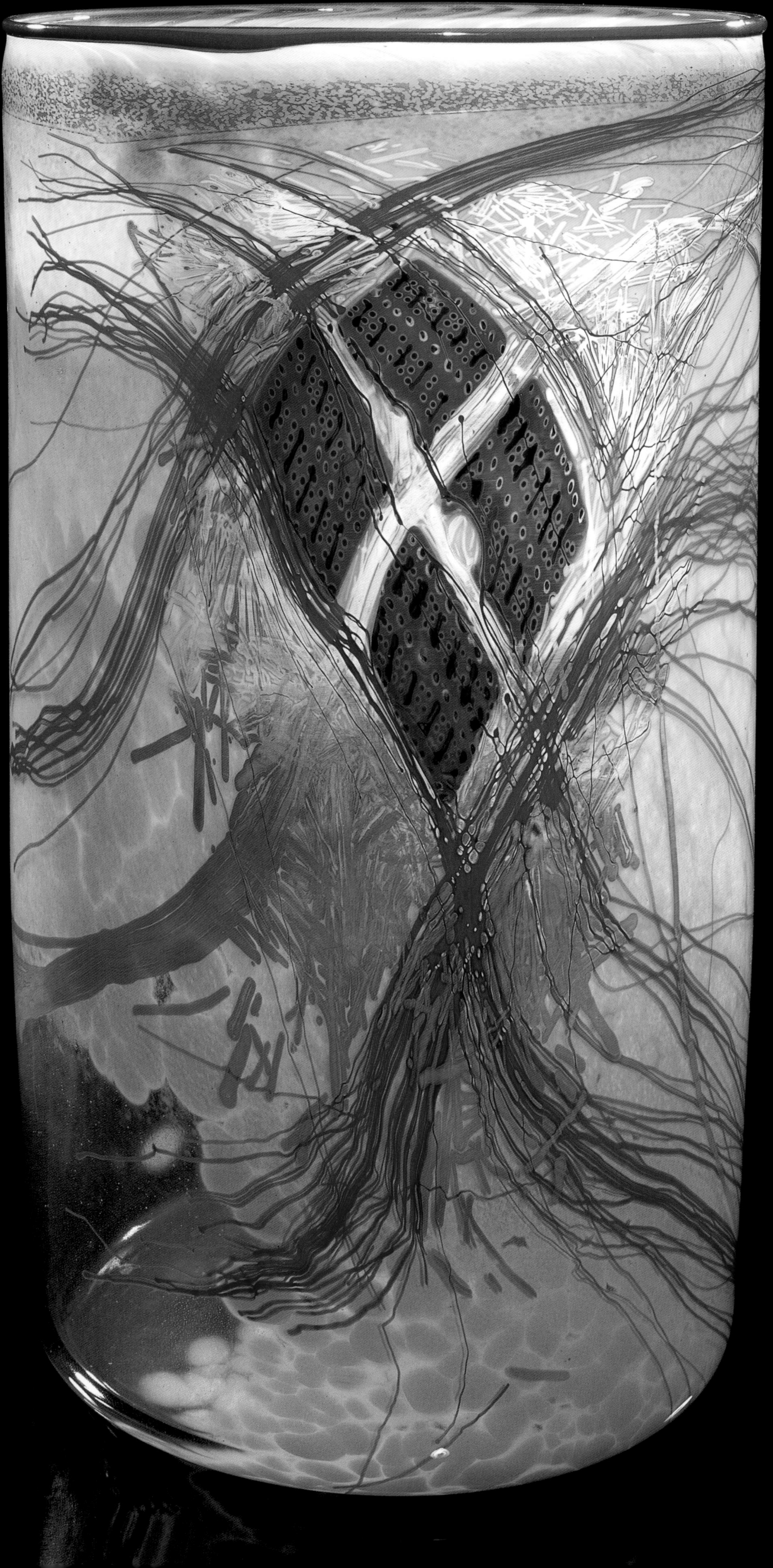

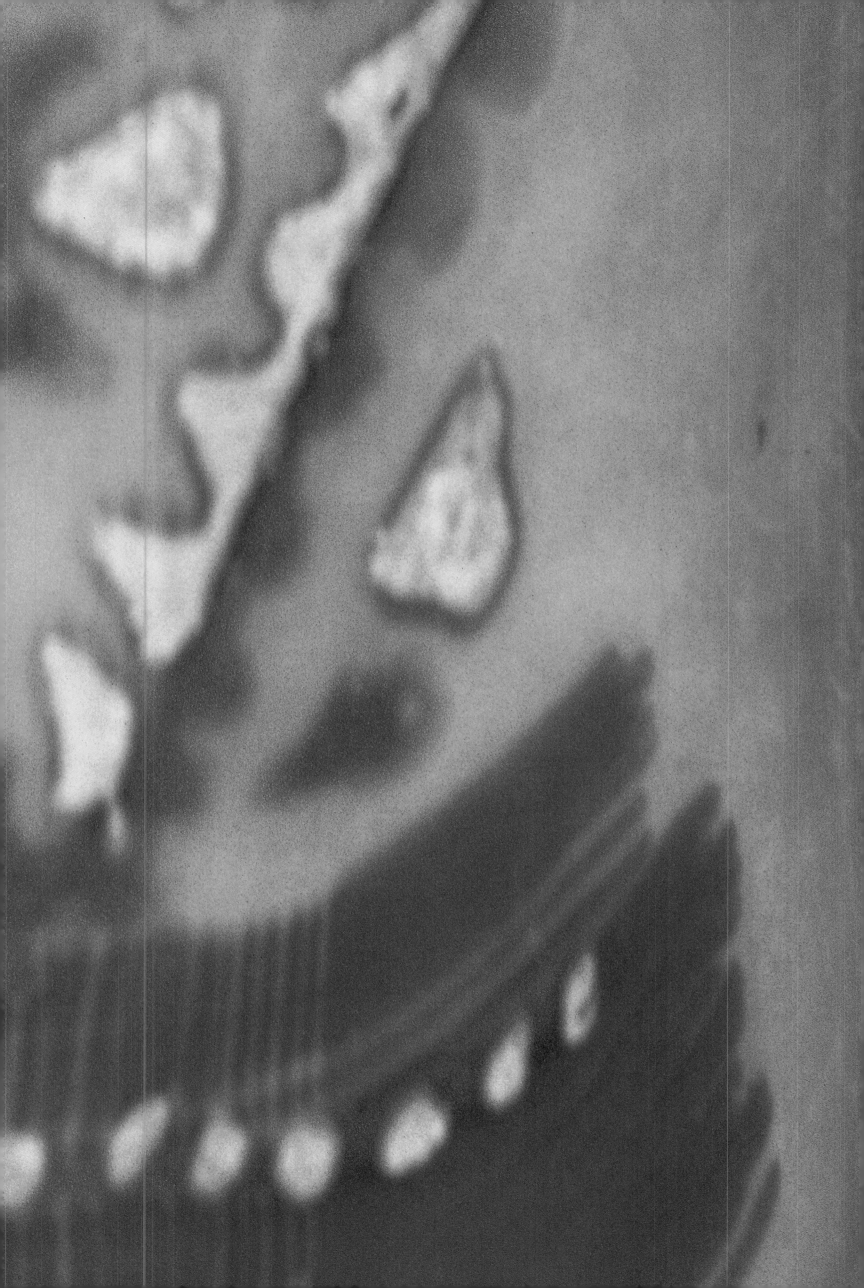

209

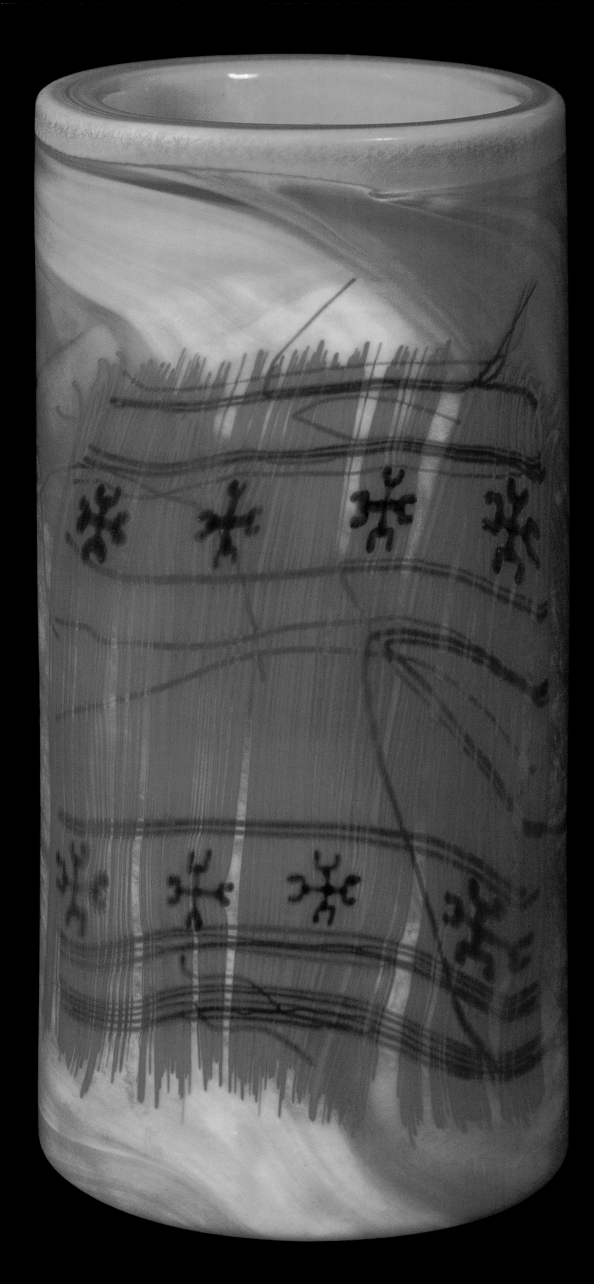

211

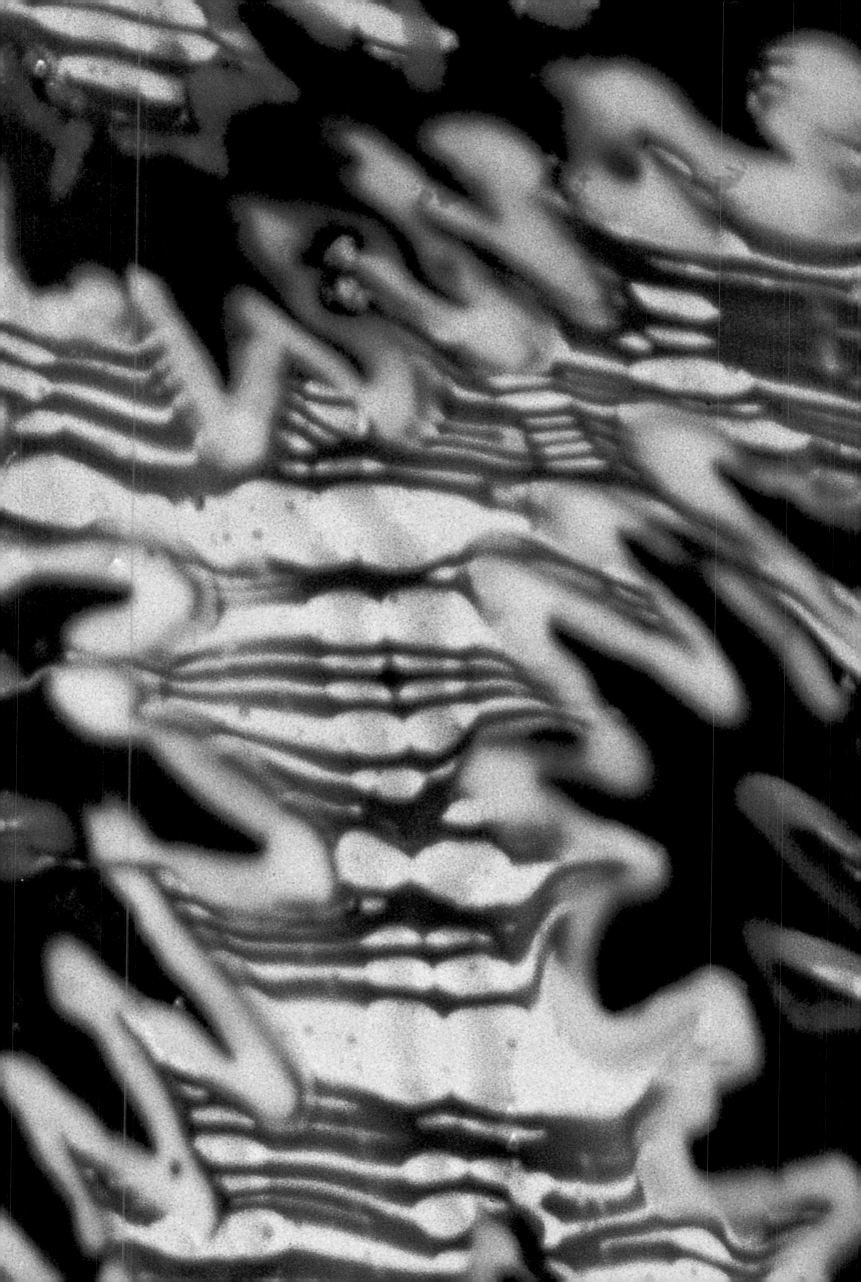

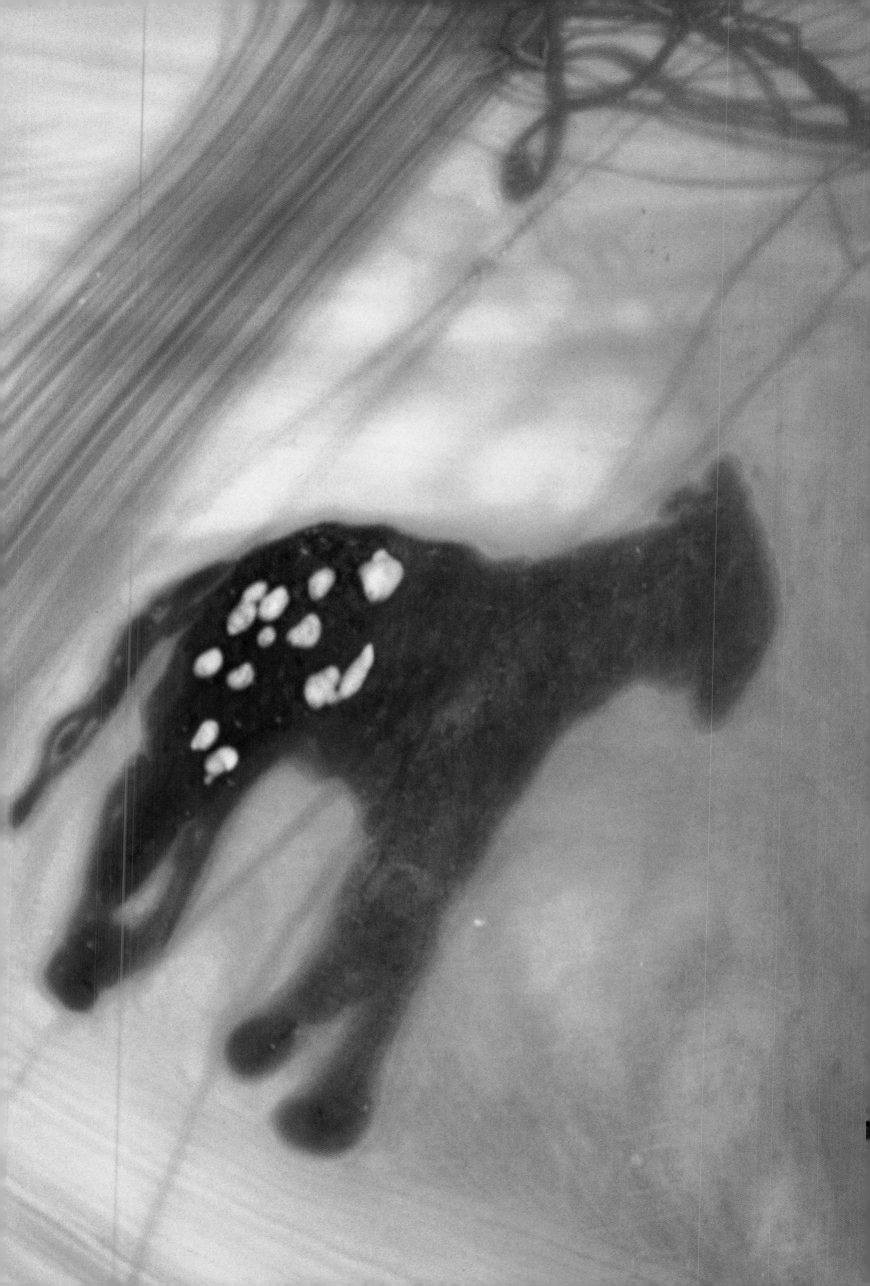

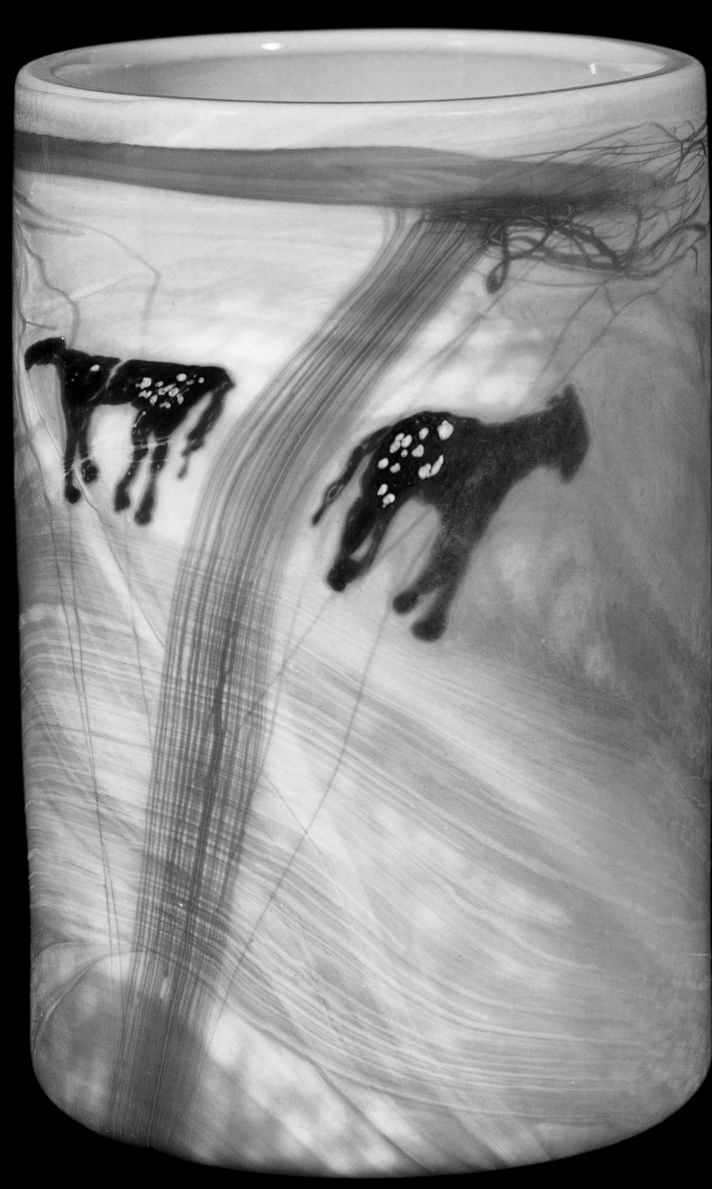

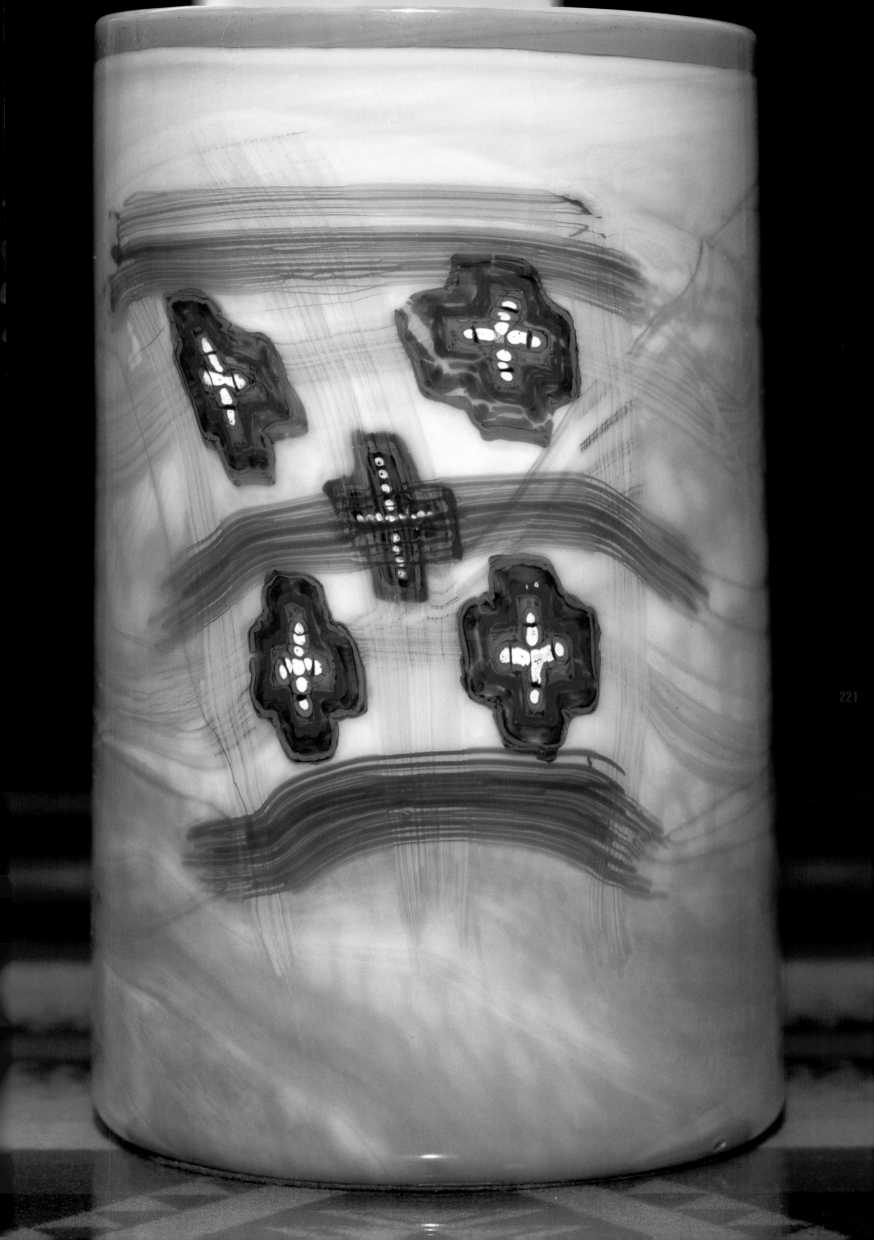

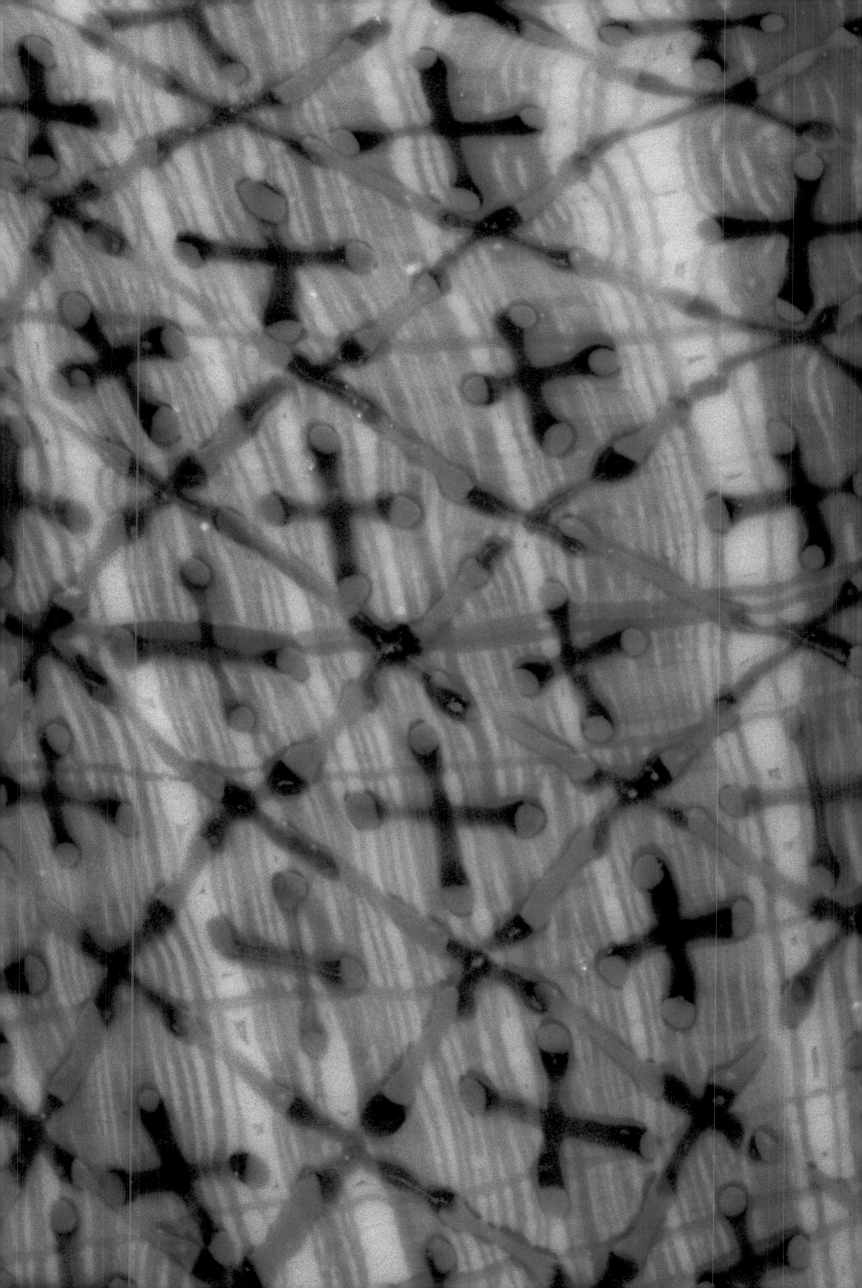

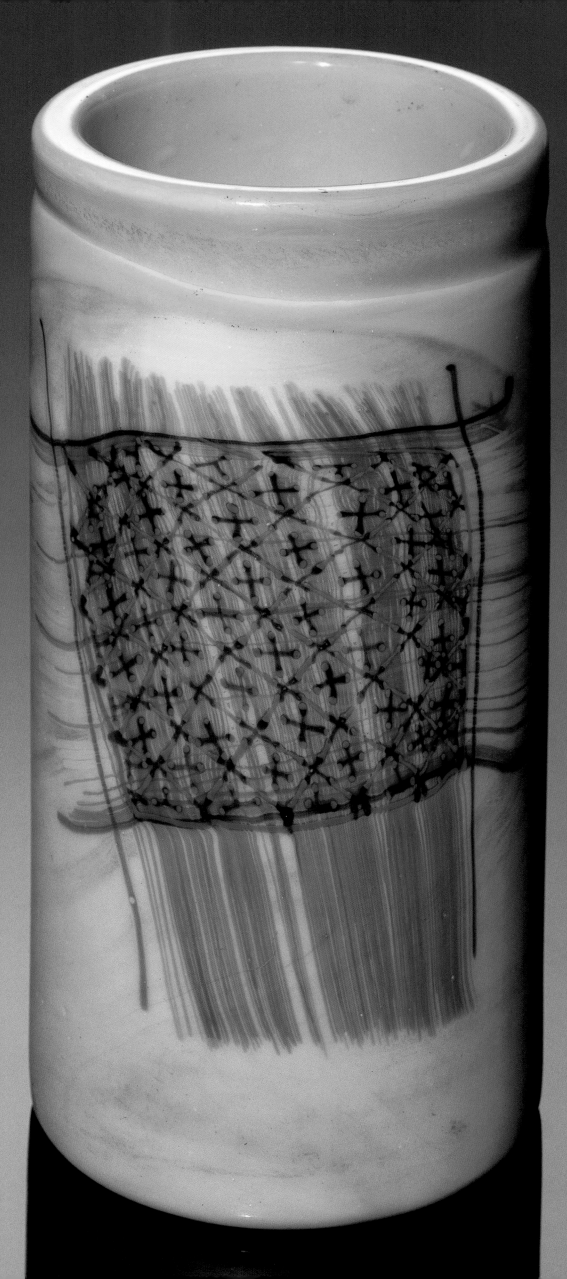

225

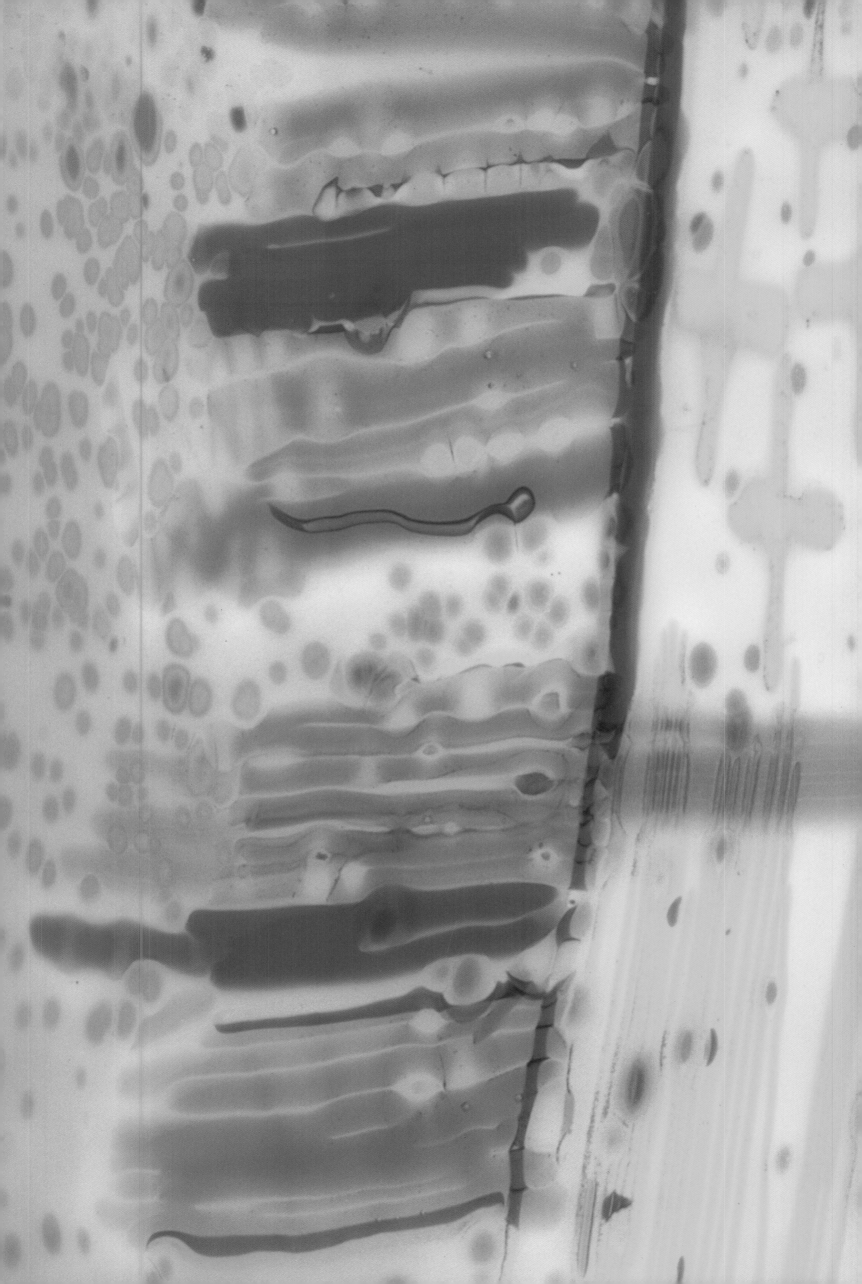

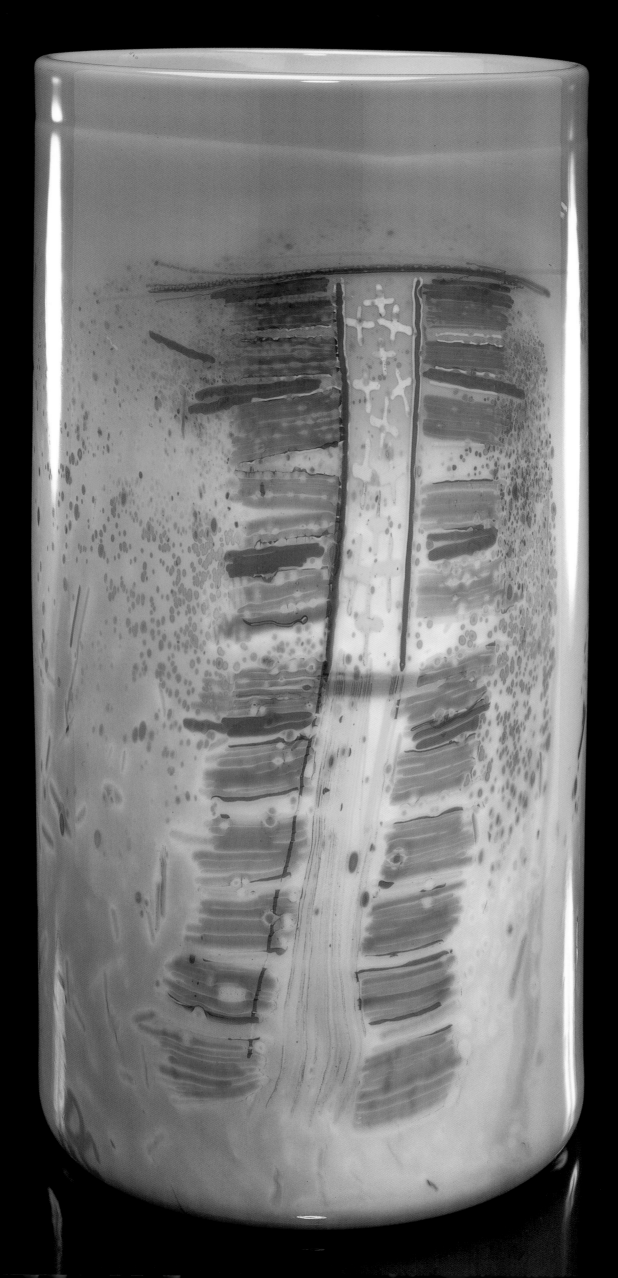

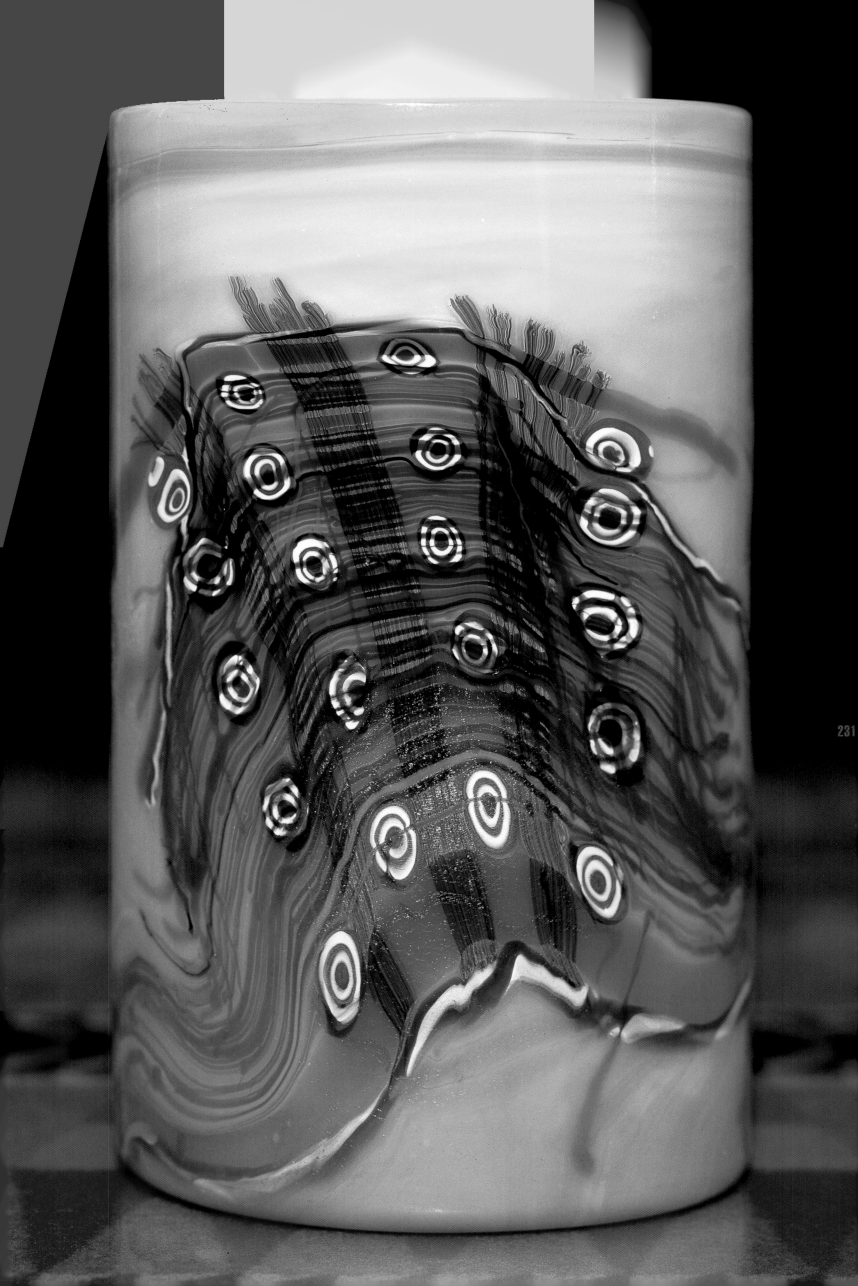

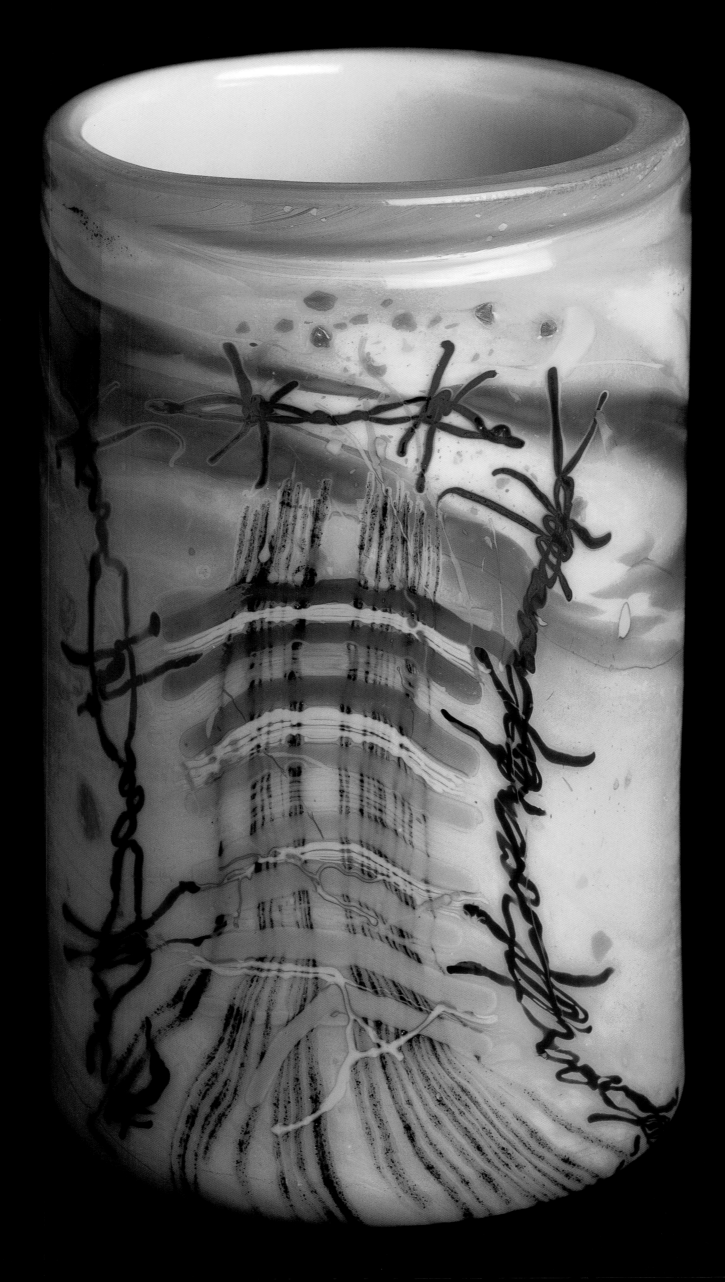

233

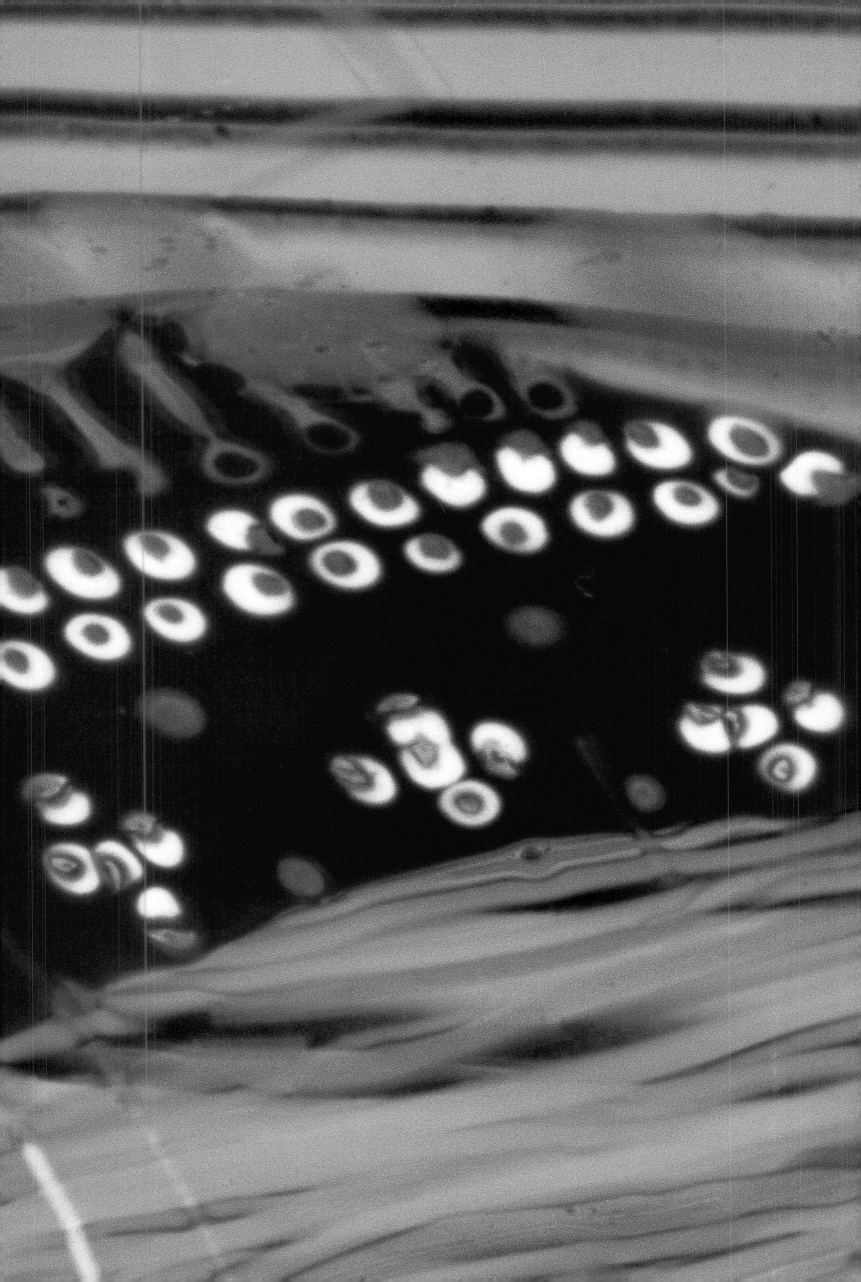

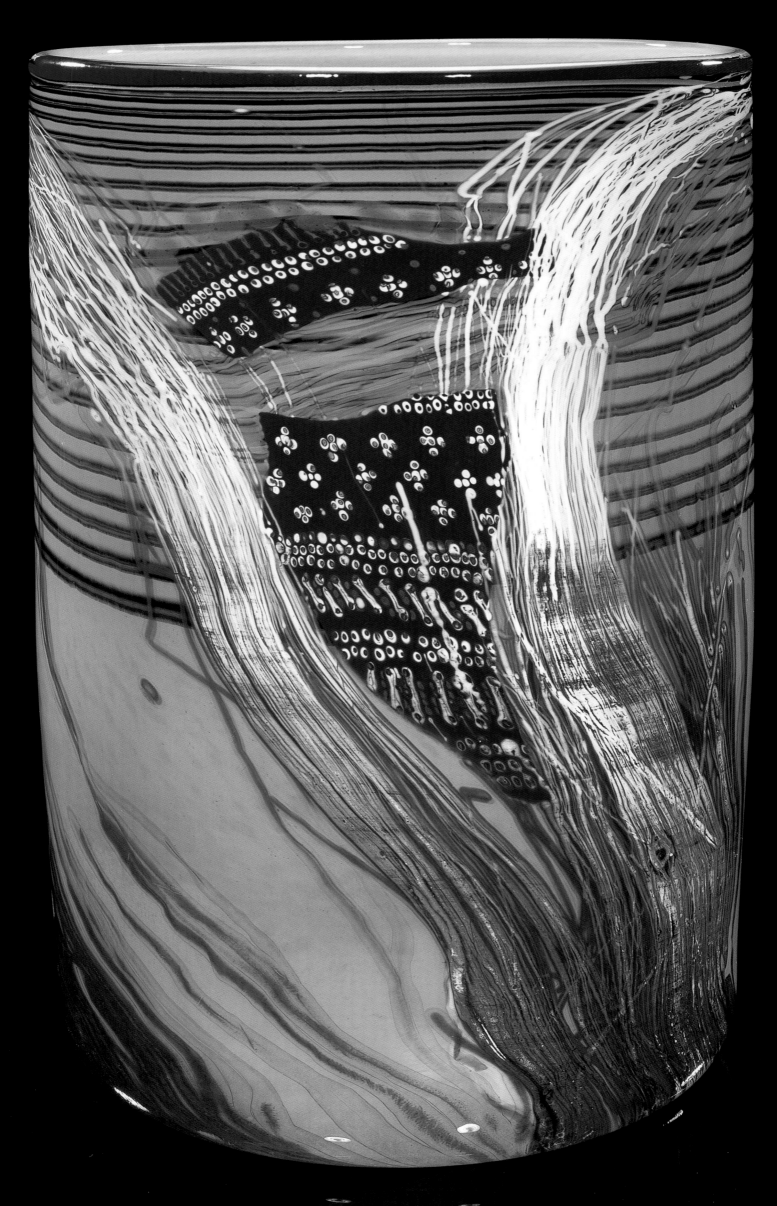

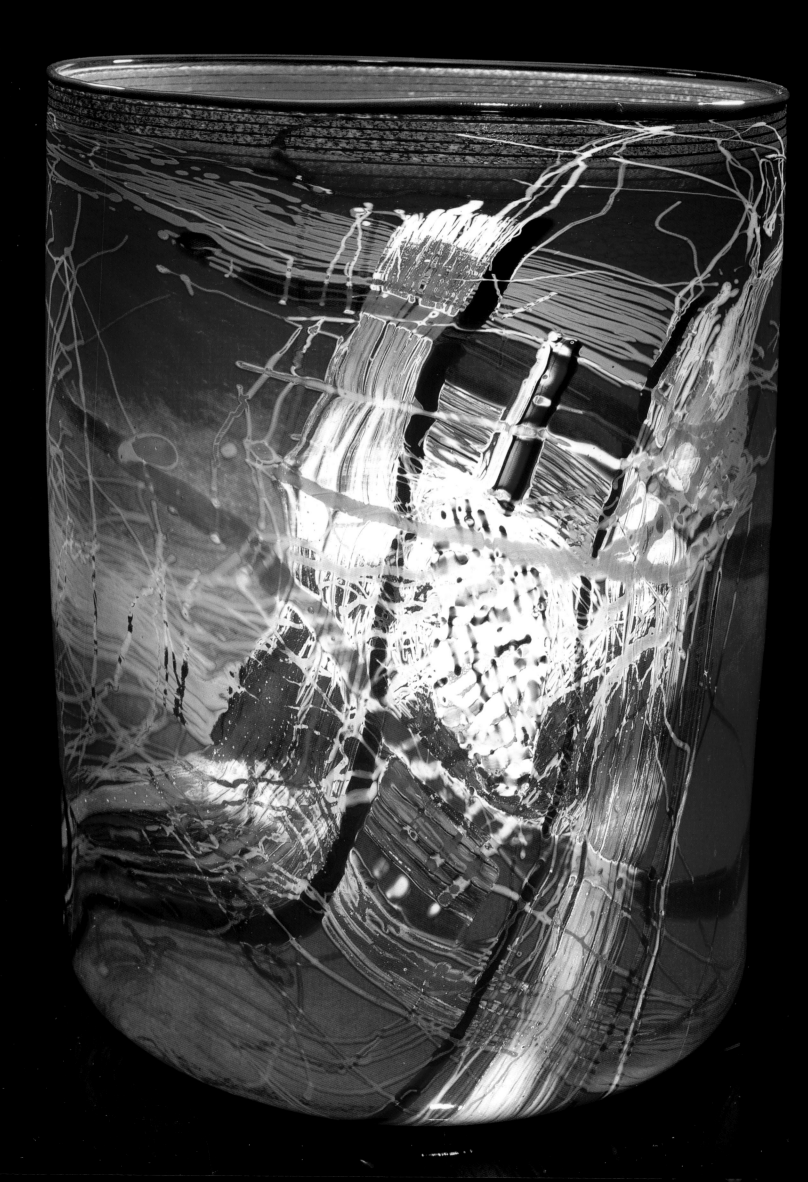

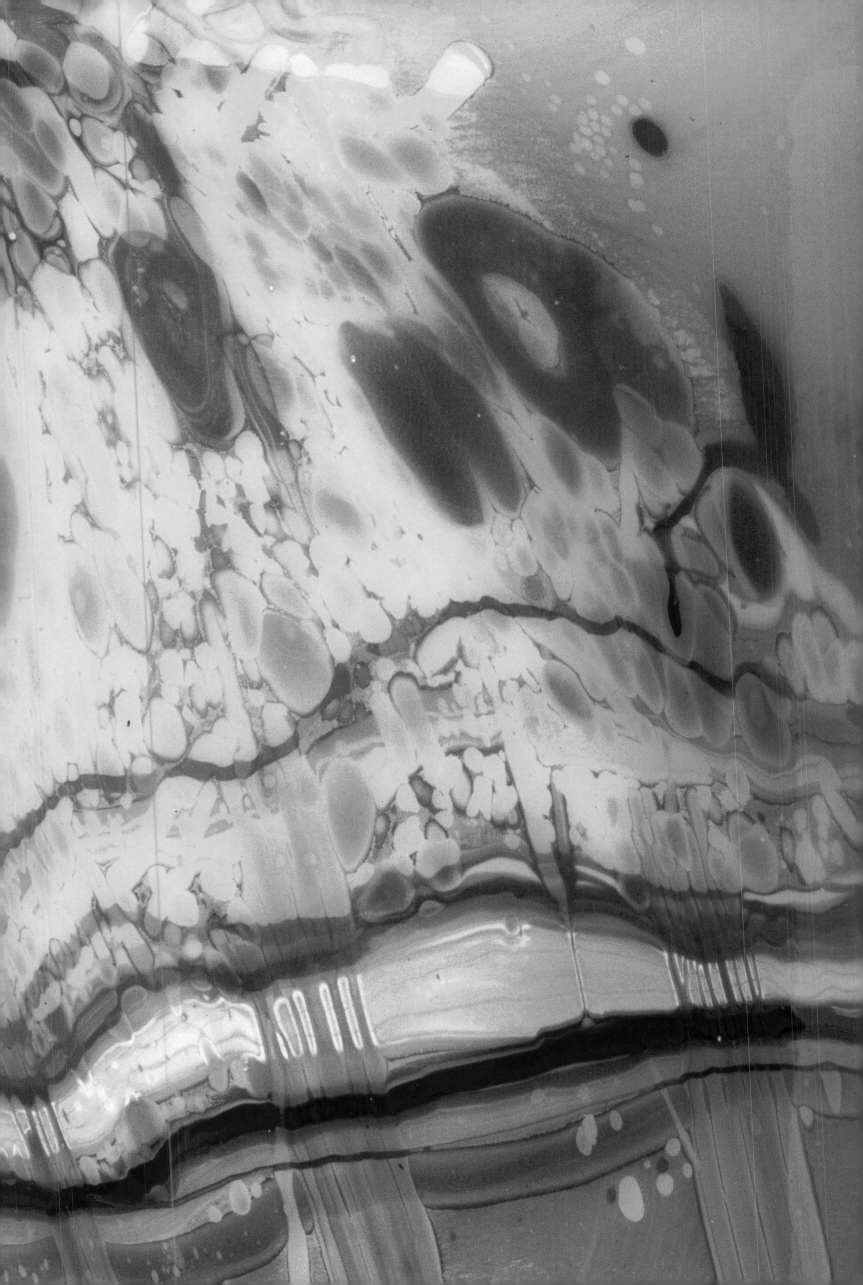

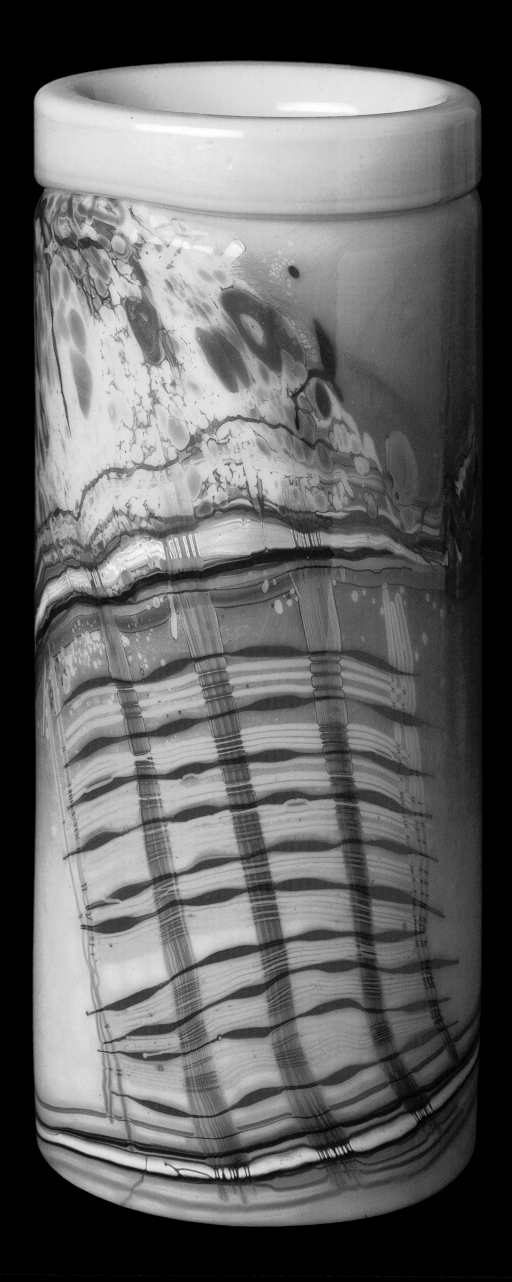

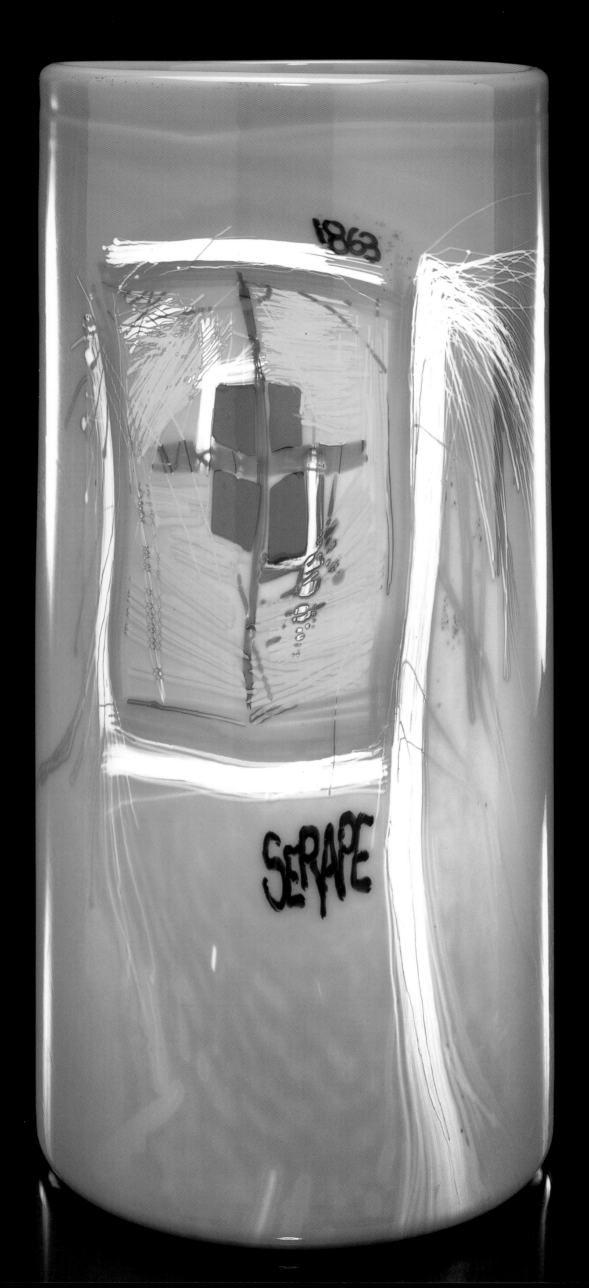

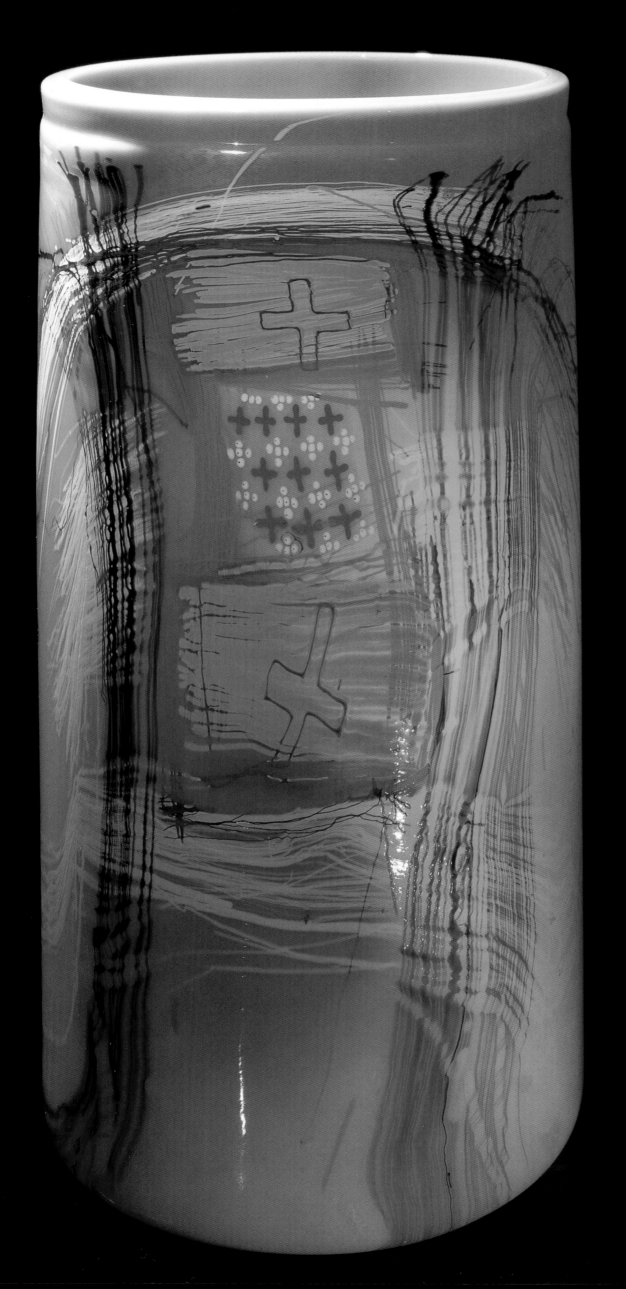

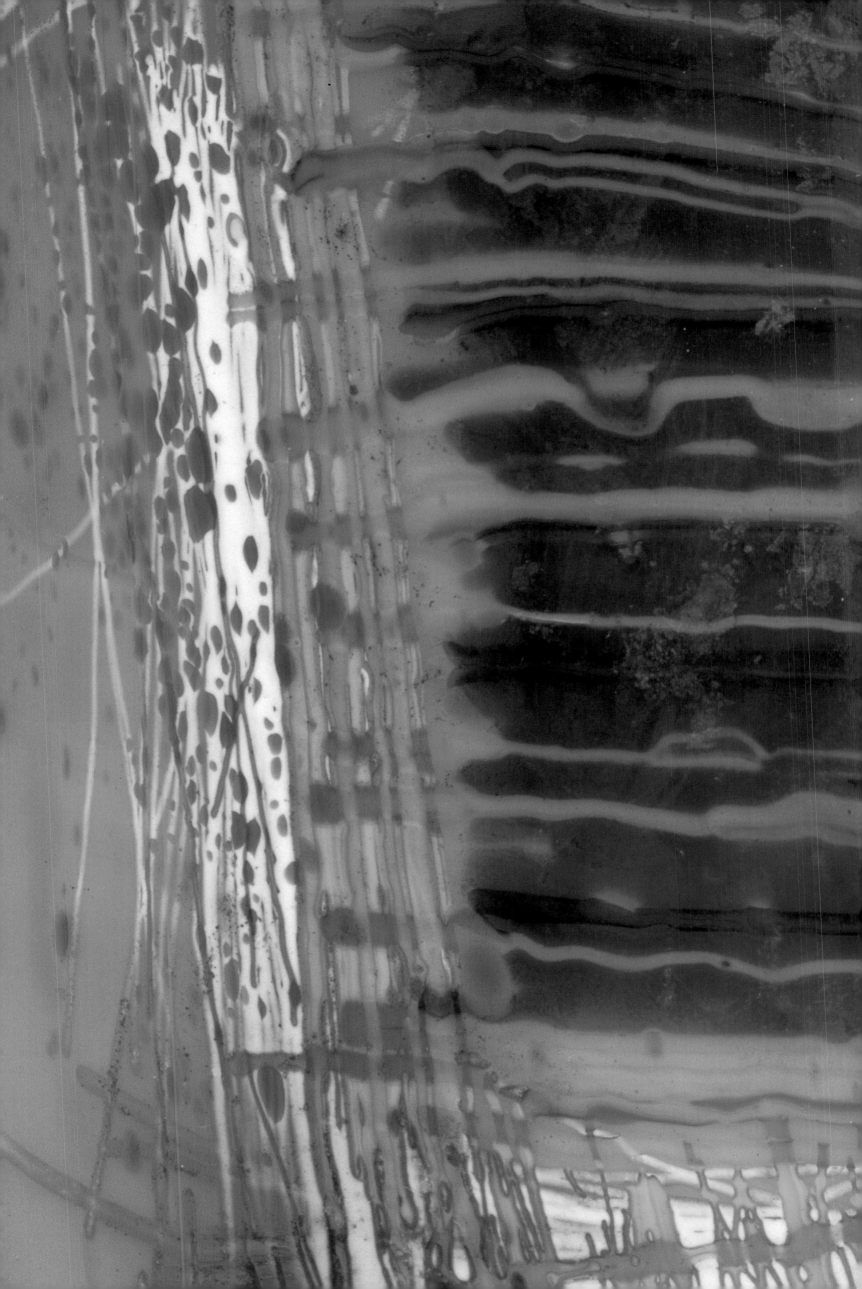

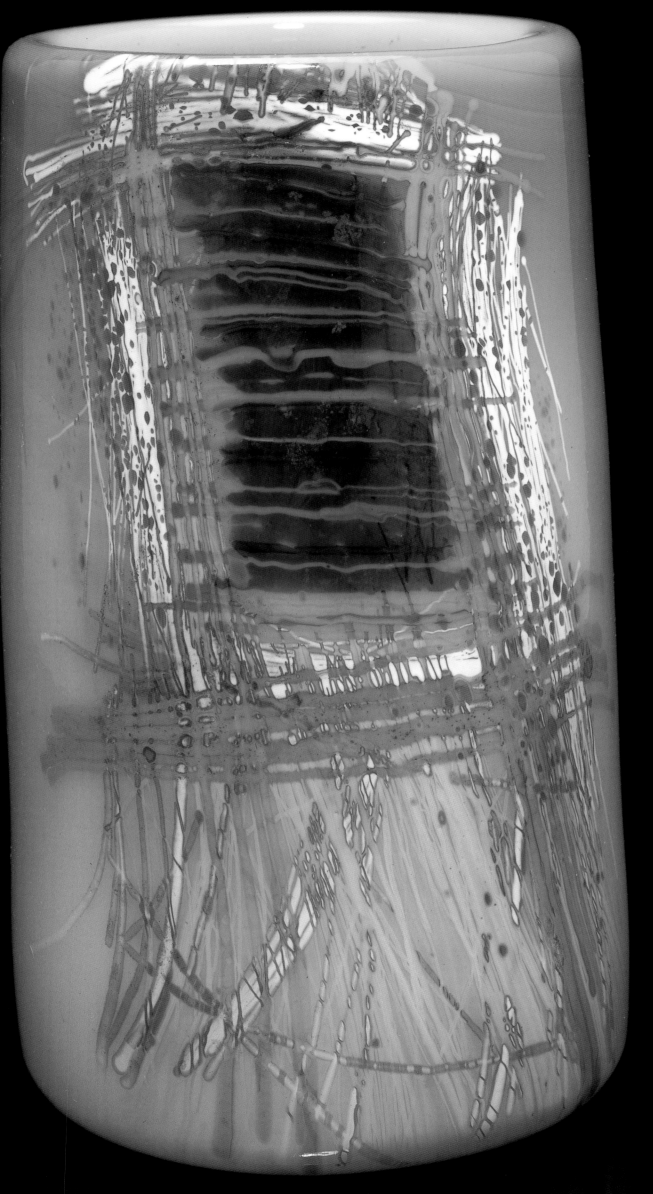

CHECKLIST

Blankets

8
Pendleton Woolen Mills, ca. 1920
Banded woman's shawl, green background, green and red overall print, red fringe.

11
Manufacturer unknown, ca. 1900
Bow, arrow, and tomahawk pictorial. Red background with four-color fringe.

16–17
Pendleton Woolen Mills, ca. 1910
Overall green, yellow, and brown pattern.

18–19
J. Capps and Sons, ca. 1913
Arapahoe Arrowhead robe. Green background with yellow, red, and brown pattern, red binding.

20–21
Buell Manufacturing Co., ca. 1890–1900s
Tan-banded, multi-design, Backgammon pattern.

22–23
Buell Manufacturing Co., ca. 1912
Green, orange, black, yellow, and beige pattern (birds), stitch binding. Comanche design.

28–29
Pendleton Woolen Mills, ca. 1920
Center Point orange and brown framed pattern.

30–31
Pendleton Woolen Mills, ca. 1920
Nine Element shawl with yellow background, green, black, and beige pattern, yellow fringe. Yakima pattern.

32–33
Oregon City Woolen Mills, ca. 1920
Woman's shawl, fringe cropped, overall pattern.

34–35, 37
Oregon City Woolen Mills, ca. 1920
Banded center-patterned shawl, tan fringe.

39
Pendleton Woolen Mills, ca. 1900
Nine Element banded gray, black, beige, and olive green overall pattern, green felt binding.

40–41
Oregon City Woolen Mills, ca. 1920
Wool, overall pattern, felt binding worn off.

42–43
Oregon City Woolen Mills, ca. 1923
Red-orange background, banded pattern with red, purple, yellow, green, and brown, red-orange felt binding.

44–45
Oregon City Woolen Mills, ca. 1914
Center Point design, brown background, beige and red overall pattern, stitched binding.

46–47
Pendleton Woolen Mills, ca. 1910
Red Tepee pattern couch cover.

48–49
Pendleton Woolen Mills, ca. 1920s–1930s
Green Center Point robe.

50–51
Pendleton Woolen Mills, ca. 1920
Black Center Point shawl with multicolored stripes and diamond along edges, black fringe.

52–53
Pendleton Woolen Mills, ca. 1920s
Black Six Element robe.

54–55
Racine Woolen Mills, ca. 1900–1910
Banded pattern, dark background.

56–57
Racine Woolen Mills, ca. 1890s
Banded style.

58–59
Pendleton Woolen Mills, ca. 1920
Frame design, blue background, red felt binding.

60–61
Oregon City Woolen Mills, ca. 1920
Banded teal background with pink, light brown, beige, and black pattern, beige stitch binding.

62–63
Pendleton Woolen Mills, ca. 1930s
Banded woman's shawl.

64–65
Oregon City Woolen Mills, ca. 1911
Overall pink background, beige stitch binding on sides, beige binding on ends.

67
Pendleton Woolen Mills, ca. 1920
Light purple background with green, red, and pink stripes, green felt binding.

68–69
Buell Manufacturing Co., ca. 1912
Banded pattern with olive green. Third Phase Chief's design.

70
Pendleton Woolen Mills, ca. 1910
Overall black, gray, beige, red,
and green pattern, black binding.

72–73
Pendleton Woolen Mills, ca. 1920
Nine Element tan background,
orange fringe.

74–75
Pendleton Woolen Mills, ca. 1920
Dark olive Cayuse shawl with tan,
red, and green pattern, olive fringe.

76–77
J. Capps and Sons, ca. 1913
Moqui robe. Tan background with
salmon, yellow, peach, and dark
brown pattern, brown binding.

80–81
Manufacturer unknown
Couch cover. Salmon background
with black, peach, and green
stripes, old pink binding.

82–83
Oregon City Woolen Mills, ca. 1926
Nine Element design. Green background
with orange, red, black, cream and gray
pattern, green binding.

84–85
Pendleton Woolen Mills, ca. 1920
Nine Element design, woman's shawl.

86–87
Pendleton Woolen Mills, ca. 1915–21
Red framed robe.

88–89
Pendleton Woolen Mills, ca. 1896–1904
Banded, round corners.

90–91
Pendleton Woolen Mills, ca. 1920s
Overall pattern.

92–93
Manufacturer unknown, ca. 1900
Banded olive background with orange,
yellow, red, and purple pattern, round
corners, red binding.

94–95
Pendleton Woolen Mills, ca. 1900
Banded red-orange background with
brown, green, orange, and yellow
pattern, round corners.

98–99
Manufacturer unknown, ca. 1900
Green background with red, purple,
and beige pattern, all-around
multicolored fringe.

100–101
Manufacturer unknown, ca. 1900
Banded lime background with
multicolored pattern, red binding.

102–103
Buell Manufacturing Co., ca. 1912
Light green with black, yellow,
and red. Zuni design.

108–109
Buell Manufacturing Co., ca. 1912
Yellow and green Nine Element
Cheyenne blanket.

110–111
J. Capps and Sons, ca. 1910
Bent Cross overall pattern with gold
background, dark brown felt binding.

112–113
Pendleton Woolen Mills, ca. 1930
Banded red background with blue
and red pattern.

114–115
Racine Woolen Mills, ca. 1912
Banded blue robe.

116–117
Manufacturer unknown, ca. 1900
Banded purple background with green,
yellow, and red star/diamond pattern,
red binding.

118
Pendleton Woolen Mills, ca. 1910
Overall pattern.

122–123
J. Capps and Sons, ca. 1912
Banded teal background, with yellow,
black, orange, and teal pattern, red
binding.

124–125
Buell Manufacturing Co., ca. 1900
Pink with green, black, and cream
pattern, lime green binding.

126–127
Pendleton Woolen Mills, ca. 1910
Overall orange, green, beige, and
dark olive pattern, old stitch binding.

130
Pendleton Woolen Mills, ca. 1920
Framed Center Point, brown
background with multicolored stripes,
brown fringe.

135–136
Oregon City Woolen Mills, ca. 1920
Center Point banded design.
Tan background with red, yellow, and
turquoise pattern, brown binding.

140–141
Pendleton Woolen Mills, ca. 1910
Banded pink robe.

142–143
Pendleton Woolen Mills, ca. 1920s
Banded Style Robe.

144–145
Buell Manufacturing Co., ca. 1912
Overall olive green, orange, yellow,
and black pattern, stitch binding.
Aztec design.

148–149
Oregon City Woolen Mills, ca. 1920s
Green Six Element robe.

150, 152–153
Pendleton Woolen Mills, ca. 1921
Nine Element robe.

156–157
Pendleton Woolen Mills, ca. 1920
Beige background with yellow,
orange, red, mint green, and black
pattern, gold binding.

158–159
Oregon City Woolen Mills, ca. 1914
Green background with burgundy
and tan Bent Cross pattern.

160–163
Racine Woolen Manfacturing Co., ca. 1912
Badger State framed, red-striped shawl.

165, 166–167
J. Capps and Sons, ca. 1912
Banded brown robe.
Shoshone pattern.

Indians

4
Jemez Pueblo, 1912
Courtesy of The Museum of
New Mexico, Neg. #61712

14–15
Bear Dance at Ouray Agency, 1891
Courtesy of The Colorado Springs
Pioneers Museum

24–25
Property of the Division of
Special Collection and University
Archives, Courtesy of the
University of Oregon Library
System, Neg. #CN1392

26–27
Courtesy of The Denver
Public Libraries, Western
History Department

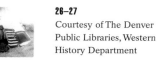

36
Courtesy of The Special Collections,
University of Washington Libraries,
Neg. #4884

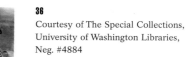

38
Cochiti Pueblo, 1920
Photo by T. Harmon Parkhurst,
Courtesy of The Museum of
New Mexico, Neg. #44590

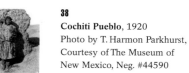

66
Courtesy of The Museum of
History and Industry, Seattle,
Washington

70
Courtesy of The Washington
State Historical Society

78–79
Wichita Indians at the payment of
January 1900 January 16, 1901
Courtesy of The Western History
Collections, University of
Oklahoma Library

96–97
Courtesy of The Special Collections,
University of Washington Libraries,
Neg. #1296

104–105
Kuhn, Soule, and McMillan
Collection. Courtesy Tacoma
Public Library, Neg. #KU15

106
Adelano Montoya, San Ildefonso
Pueblo, at Otowi, New Mexico
Courtesy of The Museum of
New Mexico, Neg. #47532

107
Courtesy of Cheyenne Cowles
Museum / Eastern Washington
State Historical Society,
Spokane, Washington

119
Lorenzo Herrera and wife
Abenita and children
Cochita Pueblo, ca.1917
Photo by T. Harmon Parkhurst
Courtesy of The Museum of New
Mexico, Neg. #9219

120–121
Group of Navajos in Morning Prayer
Courtesy of Colorado Historical
Society, Neg. #33,330

146–147
Courtesy of University of
Oregon Library

151
Patricio Calabaza and Rafael
Labota, Santo Domingo Pueblo
Photo by Witter Bynner, 1930
Courtesy of The Museum
of New Mexico, Neg. #93836

154
Navajo man, 1935
Photo by T. Harmon Parkhurst,
Courtesy of The Museum
of New Mexico, Neg. #89800

155
San Ildefonso Pueblo, ca.1915
Photo by Jesse L. Nusbaum,
Courtesy of The Museum
of New Mexico, Neg. #61777

164
Special Collections Division,
Courtesy of the University of
Washington Libraries, Neg. #609

168
Fish Hawk, 1935
Courtesy of The Burke Museum
of Natural History and Culture

169
Hopi, AZ, ca. 1911
Photo by H.F. Robinson,
Courtesy of The Museum
of New Mexico, Neg. #36020

170
Santo Domingo Pueblo, 1935
Photo by T. Harmon Parkhurst
Courtesy of The Museum of
New Mexico, Neg. #47222

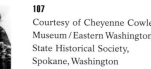

171
Santo Domingo Pueblo, 1935
Courtesy of The Museum of
New Mexico, Neg. #28924

Cylinders

172
Early Fused Glass Weaving, 1965
35 x 24 x 4"

195
Indian Blanket Cylinders with
Blanket Drawings, 1975
7 x 4" (left), 9 x 6" (right)

197
Woven Horse Blanket Cylinder, 1978
11 x 6 x 6"

199
Indian Pony Cylinder, 1976
11 x 5.5 x 5.5"

201
Peach Cylinder with
Indian Blanket Drawing, 1995
17.5 x 6 x 6"

203
Indian Blanket Cylinder
with Drawing, 1980
11 x 8 x 8"

205
1883 Indian Cylinder, 1975
12 x 5 x 5"

207
Peach Cylinder with
Ruby Lip Wrap, 1984
17.5 x 9.5 x 9.5"

209
1976
13" high

211
Indian Blanket Cylinder with
Cross Blanket Drawing, 1975
11.5 x 6 x 6"

213
Peach Cylinder with
Blanket Drawing, 1975
9 x 6 x 6"

215
Bottle Green Zig Zag
Blanket Cylinder, 1976
11 x 8 x 8"

217
Peach Cylinder with
Blanket Drawing, 1973
9 x 6.5 x 6.5"

219
Jumping Horses Cylinder
12 x 6 x 6"

221
Five Cross Cylinder, 1976
15 x 7 x 7"

223
Twelve Cross Cylinder, 1976
12 x 5.5 x 5.5"

225
Blanket Cylinder with
White Threads, 1975
11.5 x 6 x 6"

227
Peach Cylinder with Indian
Blanket Drawing, 1995
12 x 7 x 7"

229
Peach Cylinder with Indian
Blanket Drawing, 1995
18 x 9 x 9"

231
Winter Blanket, 1976
11 x 6 x 6"

233
Indian Blanket Cylinder with
Woven Blanket Drawing, 1976
14 x 7.5 x 7.5"

235
Pink Cylinder with Cobalt Blue
Lip Wrap, 1984
14 x 10 x 9"

237
Silver Gray Soft Cylinder with
Deep Green Lip Wrap, 1982
17 x 13.5 x 13"

239
Cylinder with Blanket
Drawing, 1975
14 x 5.5 x 5.5"

241
Peach Cylinder with Indian
Blanket Drawing, 1995
20 x 9 x 9"

243
Peach Cylinder with Indian
Blanket Drawing, 1995
16 x 8 x 8"

245
Peach Cylinder with Indian
Blanket Drawing, 1995
7 x 4 x 4"

This first edition of *Chihuly's Pendletons*
is limited to 15,000 casebound copies.
The entire contents are copyright © 2000 Dale Chihuly.
All Rights Reserved

Photographs:
Ira Garber
Claire Garoutte
Donna Goetsch
Art Huppy
Russell Johnson
Scott M. Leen
Teresa Rishel
Roger Schreiber
Chuck Taylor

Design: Malcolm Grear Designers
Typefaces: Rotation and Swiss 911 Compressed
Paper: Silk Art matt 157 gsm

Printed in Hong Kong and bound in China by C & C Offset
Distributed by University of Arizona Press

Portland Press

P. O. Box 45010

Seattle, Washington 98143

800-574-7272

www.portlandpress.net

ISBN 1-57684-015-8